WITHDRAWN
NDSU

INSTITUTE OF INTERNATIONAL STUDIES
YALE UNIVERSITY

The Super-Powers

**THE UNITED STATES, BRITAIN,
AND THE SOVIET UNION—
THEIR RESPONSIBILITY FOR PEACE**

The Yale Institute of International Studies was organized in 1935 for the purpose of promoting research and postgraduate training in the field of international relations. Although concerned with all aspects of international affairs, its research program is devoted primarily to studies designed to clarify contemporary problems in the foreign policy of the United States. In 1938 the Institute published "The Far Eastern Policy of the United States" by A. Whitney Griswold, and in 1940 a history of the development of modern American naval policy by George T. Davis entitled "A Navy Second to None." In the same year appeared a volume by Arnold Wolfers called "Britain and France between Two Wars," a study of the respective peace strategies of the two countries. In 1942 the Institute published a volume by Nicholas John Spykman, its first director, called "America's Strategy in World Politics," an analysis of the position of the United States in relation to the balance of power in Europe and Asia. An historical interpretation of United States relations with Latin America by Samuel Flagg Bemis was published in 1943 under the title "The Latin American Policy of the United States." The most recent publication of the Institute is a posthumous volume by Nicholas John Spykman on "The Geography of the Peace," issued in April, 1944, a geopolitical study of world politics during the war and in the peace to come.

Frederick Sherwood Dunn, Director

THE
Super-Powers

*THE UNITED STATES, BRITAIN, AND
THE SOVIET UNION —
THEIR RESPONSIBILITY FOR PEACE*

BY

WILLIAM T. R. FOX

RESEARCH ASSOCIATE,
YALE INSTITUTE OF INTERNATIONAL STUDIES

HARCOURT, BRACE AND COMPANY, *New York*

COPYRIGHT, 1944, BY
HARCOURT, BRACE AND COMPANY, INC.

All rights reserved, including the right to reproduce this book or portions thereof in any form.

first edition

D
825
F64

A WARTIME BOOK
This complete edition is produced in full compliance with the government's regulations for conserving paper and other essential materials.

PRINTED IN THE UNITED STATES OF AMERICA

Acknowledgments

ALTHOUGH working on individual projects, the members of the Yale Institute of International Studies carry on their research in close association. This has permitted a free and constant interchange of ideas from which I have been a major beneficiary. I am especially indebted to the Institute's director, Frederick Sherwood Dunn, for the opportunity to write this book and for his friendly but frank criticism at each stage of the work. The manuscript has also benefited from the criticism of Percy E. Corbett, Jacob Viner, and Arnold Wolfers and from that of my wife, Annette Baker Fox, in her capacity as a political scientist. The fruitful conceptions of Harold D. Lasswell, Sigmund Neumann, David N. Rowe, and Harold Sprout have contributed to the formulation of important parts of this book. To Helen R. Nicholl credit is due for the elimination of many rough spots in the original composition. It is a pleasure to record the competent and enthusiastic research assistance of Emily Wilson Rabe. For the careful typing of the manuscript I am indebted to Veronica E. O'Neill and her assistants, Jean Collier and Marcella Davis. Responsibility for errors in fact or interpretation which the efforts of all those mentioned above were unsuccessful in eliminating remains of course with me.

For permission to quote from works published by them I am indebted to the Harvard University Press; Houghton Mifflin Company; Little, Brown and Company; Oxford University Press; Princeton University Press; and the publishers of *American Journal of International Law, Belgium, Christian Century, Foreign Affairs,* and *Journal of Politics.* Explanatory footnotes have been placed in the text, and bibliographical notes and references on pp. 165-73.

WILLIAM T. R. FOX

Contents

PART ONE
THE WORLD OF THE SUPER-POWERS

I. In Defense of Talking About Power ... 3
II. The Custodians of Greatest Power ... 12

PART TWO
BRITAIN AND AMERICA

III. Britain vs. America ... 27
IV. Strategic Interdependence ... 50

PART THREE
THE WESTERN POWERS AND THE SOVIET UNION

V. Forecasting Soviet Policy ... 73
VI. The Price of Collaboration and the Consequences of Noncollaboration ... 92

PART FOUR
THE AGENDA OF COLLABORATION

VII. Germany and the New Europe ... 109
VIII. The Economy of Joint Action ... 129
IX. The Super-Powers and the World Community ... 140
X. Coalition for Peace: a Program for Our Own Time ... 156

Notes ... 165
Index ... 177

PART ONE

THE WORLD OF THE SUPER-POWERS

I. In Defense of Talking About Power

> *Even after you give the squirrel a certificate which says he is quite as big as any elephant, he is still going to be smaller, and all the squirrels will know it and all the elephants will know it.*
> SAMUEL GRAFTON in the New York *Post*, November 23, 1943.

THIS is a book about the high politics of the postwar world. It pays special attention to the elephants, but not because they have a moral right to exist and to do as they please which is superior to the moral right of the squirrels to do the same. In a well-ordered world there will be room for both elephants and squirrels, and both will live in an atmosphere of security never known in our own time. This well-ordered world is within our grasp, but we will never reach it by ignoring the differences between the elephants and the squirrels of international politics.

We can of course, if we wish, construct an imaginary world in which there are no elephants; and it will be true that in that world of make-believe the great-power aggressors will not have to be restrained by great-power defenders of the *status quo*. But we will be doing a great disservice to a war-weary world if we pretend that the world in which there are no elephants is a world which will actually exist in the very near future or that it is the world we are fighting for. The Soviet Union and the Dominican Republic are not both elephants, nor are they both squirrels; and we are not fighting to make them both squirrels.

The Western state system has always been dominated by a few great states. Out of the chaos of the Thirty Years' War there emerged a Europe whose political life was ordered by a select coterie of the more powerful who recognized each other as "The Great Powers." It is altogether likely that man must, in the future as in the past, guard against the menace of arbitrary power. Because some states have great power and others have much less, there will always be the danger that the government of some great power will see in that difference an opportunity for cheap and profitable aggression. But power can be used to protect as well as to enslave.[1] In the world we are going to have to live in, differences in power do and will exist. Our problem is to discover the conditions of security in that world. A blueprint for peace which posits the disappearance of all the great powers must be labeled: "No solution." It is only a blueprint for the utopia in which some of us would like to dwell.

To say that armed power is responsible for our present miseries is like saying that, because the large intestine is a favorite breeding-ground for many germs, it is the chief cause of disease. Health cannot be assured by removing the large intestine, nor can peace by legislating armed power out of existence.[2]

When men in their daily conversation refer to states as "great powers" or as "small powers," they testify to the importance of the possession of power. Trends in the distribution of power among nations largely determine the evolution of the pattern of international relationships, because the possibility of the resort to violence is never excluded. The relations of states in such a world community will in this book be called "power politics." It is a peculiarly American notion to assume that problems in a world of power politics can be solved by creating a world of no-power politics. This belief was not, however, shared by Hamilton, Jefferson, and many other early statesmen of the Republic. Their writings reveal a keen insight into the relation between American security and European power politics. Hamilton understood that with a modest naval establishment the United States would "be able to incline the balance of European competitions in this part of the world as our interest may dictate." [3]

The century of comparative peace in Europe after Waterloo obscured the vital connection between America's security and Europe's struggles. Theodore Roosevelt was perhaps the first modern American in high public office to base foreign policy on a frank recognition of the necessity for constantly calculating military-power relationships. This was no doubt what Walter Lippmann had in mind when he recently wrote that "Theodore Roosevelt had . . . the elements of a genuine foreign policy." [4] The first Roosevelt obviously and ostentatiously enjoyed making American power felt in the councils of Europe and Asia.[5] Power politics he viewed as a game, the most exciting game in the world. Like any robust American, he intended if possible to win the game, in other words to establish the United States as a power of the first rank which would have to be consulted in the crises of world politics wherever and whenever they occur. Big-game hunting in Africa was for Roosevelt, the ex-President, only a poor substitute for the game he really enjoyed playing, the game of great-power politics, which as President he had been privileged to play, and which, also as President, he had felt it his duty to win in the name of the United States.

Even the austere Henry Adams confessed to being fascinated by John Hay's efforts to construct about the American nucleus a power combination which would include Britain, Germany, and finally Russia. Hay, he thought, was attempting at the international level to do what the titans of industry were doing at home, to form a trust which would substitute monopoly for competition. The game, he felt, was less sordid when played in foreign affairs since the participant was a person acting not in his own private interest but in that of his country.[6] For

Adams too, foreign affairs was an intriguing game to be won for one's country if possible.

The American people certainly felt a pleasurable sensation because of their country's new status as a great power. It was natural for them to give willing support to their enthusiastic President in his bold adventures in world politics. Later in two world wars they discovered that power politics was not merely a game, that some governments played "for keeps," and that playing the game meant that sons and brothers and fathers had to give up their lives. They can hardly be blamed for wanting to have the United States withdraw from the game. Some advocated the "isolationist" way out of the game, which meant simply refusing to play. Others advocated the "internationalist" way out, by calling for a revision of the rules according to which units of military power would no longer be the counters of victory and defeat. Neither group exhibited the sophisticated understanding of power politics essential to providing a foreign policy for the United States in the world as it really is. Those who continued to favor America's playing the game as a game were called imperialists.*

If power politics were a game, power itself would be merely a scoring device; [7] and attainment of great power would be a relatively innocuous consequence of great wealth, great population, and a favorable geographic position. Since power politics is not a game but a central feature of the organized political life of the twentieth century, it makes the most enormous difference in whose hands predominant power rests. Those few who soberly pointed out that power politics is more than a game,

* In their *The American Spirit: A Study of the Idea of Civilization in the United States*, New York, Macmillan, 1942, pp. 578-94, Charles and Mary Beard treat the imperialist and the internationalist approaches as two manifestations of the same aberration, viz., a belief that the United States has a world mission. The Republicans launched the first crusade in 1898, the Democrats the second crusade in 1917 and in their subsequent attempt to take the United States into the League of Nations. The present war is apparently the third crusade.

that power really exists, that it is the highest task of statesmanship to harmonize conflicting power groups and to canalize armed power so that it may perform its legitimate, protective role in international affairs were called by the isolationists, "interventionists."

Americans, surrounded by visual evidence that in many ways the new is better than the old, have frequently assumed that the same is true in international politics. To many, the "Old World" system of power politics appears absolutely bad. They have therefore concentrated their attention upon discovering some totally new principle by which inter-state relations should be regulated.* Americans occasionally assert that they have discovered such a principle in the "Good Neighbor-ly" relations that characterize New World politics.[8] They may instead have demonstrated how, by moderation and tact, a great power can make its preponderant position generally palatable to its less powerful neighbors. This is no mean achievement; it does not, however, provide an escape from power politics. It may be valid totally to reject the old way, but it is invalid to do so until one understands what one is rejecting. It is especially important to understand which parts of the old system cannot be rejected because they cannot be changed. If, for example, there will be in the future as in the past a small number of great powers, each incapable of being coerced except by combinations including other great powers, a "plan" for avoiding future war which is built on a different assumption has little to contribute to the urgent task of preventing war in our time.†

---

* Margaret Mead has listed this belief that the new is better than the old, that complete demolition brings best results, as a weakness in the American cultural pattern. She does not, of course, pass judgment on this "weakness" in moral terms; but she does term this belief a weakness in weighing the survival value of our way of life in its mortal combat with the Nazi way of life. *And Keep Your Powder Dry*, New York, William Morrow, 1942, Chapter XIII, esp. pp. 218-20.

† There are some who are not interested "merely" in preventing war in our time. Thus, Walter Van Kirk, writing in the *Christian Century*, February 4,

We have said that military power itself is neither good nor bad; it is ethically neutral. It is good or bad only as it is used for good or bad purposes. We need not pause for the moment to inquire what constitutes a "good" use of power. It is enough to point out that mankind generally, outside the Axis countries, finds it good that the power position of the Soviet Union, the United States, and the British Commonwealth has improved and that these powers rather than their opponents will shortly be the custodians of preponderant power.

Fifty years from now or five hundred years from now men may have discovered a substitute for armed force in world politics. It is not too soon to start planning for that day.* To understand the international relations of the next generation, however, one needs to know the precise location of preponderant military power. This power will lie either in the hands of

1942, pp. 139-40, and speaking for what he called "the churches," opposed an Anglo-American combination of power as a basis for the coming peace in the following words: ". . . the churches know that alliances and balances of power, however nobly and benevolently conceived, become in due time punitive in character and destructive of the world's peace. . . .

"A combination of the military power and the industrial resources of England and the United States might conceivably prevent the recurrence of war for the next twenty-five or fifty years. But it would be a policeman's peace. . . . The churches, as they look toward the future, are not interested in a makeshift peace nor in a peace dubiously and only temporarily supported by the bayonets of this or that nation, separately or in union."

It is difficult to see how Mr. Van Kirk's reasoning would prevent him from opposing an alliance of all the great powers or even of all the United Nations on similar grounds.

The author believes that the present will have paid its debt to the future if it "prevents war in our time" in such a fashion that it minimizes the chance of war at some future date. The generation which is fighting today has a legitimate grievance against the past, for peace was preserved in the 1920's and 1930's in ways which could only lead to war in the 1940's.

* This is the problem to which Mortimer J. Adler addressed himself in his *How to Think About War and Peace*, New York, Simon and Schuster, 1944. According to his terminology the problem of "how to make a long truce" should be sharply distinguished from that of how to attain permanent peace. On the relation between these two problems see *infra*, the concluding chapter.

the victorious great powers or in some supra-national authority itself controlling directly a police force of world-wide jurisdiction. As a possibility for producing general security in our own time, the second alternative is of only theoretical importance. For it to materialize, the great powers would have to permit the creation of a supra-national police force strong enough to coerce any one of them and constitutionally able to do so. The Soviet Union is not, however, likely to feel that its physical security would be enhanced by permitting a supra-national agency in which it might be outvoted to possess a land army capable of defeating the Red Army. Nor will Great Britain and the United States be anxious to see a supra-national naval force brought into existence which could cut the North Atlantic life line essential to the security of both. Only if all the surviving great powers were simultaneously and collectively prepared to entrust their security to a supra-national agency with preponderant force at its command could the necessary transfer of authority take place without still another world war. Something called an international police force may or may not be created; but it may safely be predicted that there will still be American, British, and Russian armies, navies, and air forces after the present war.

The task of the peacemaker is not, therefore, to emasculate the surviving great powers. It is rather to seek a definition of the national interest of each in such terms that each will find it possible to collaborate with the others to maintain a stable and just postwar order. If one or more of the surviving great powers develops a policy of unlimited expansion or of "power for the sake of domination," the quest for all-round security will necessarily fail. What are the conditions under which this eventuality may be avoided? [9]

In periods of peace, great power and great responsibility have always gone hand in hand. In the words of Pascal, "Justice without force is impotent. Force without justice is tyrannical. We must therefore combine justice with force." When for short intervals the powerful have proven irresponsible or the responsible impotent, world order and world peace have both been the losers. Responsible but impotent France and powerful but irresponsible Germany were in the 1930's equally dangerous. America's irresponsible isolationism and League of Nations impotence also demonstrate how the sundering of power and responsibility set the stage for a second world war. Since a reincarnated League can hardly be made powerful enough in its own right, some other way must be found by which responsibility and power can be firmly joined.

If the leaders of each of the great states should come to believe that it "pays"—in terms of the values pursued by each—to use power in a moderate and responsible fashion, the prospects for continuing peace would be good. Today's student of power politics has a clear responsibility; he must discover the conditions under which such a development might occur.

One further word needs to be said in defense of a book about armed power in the postwar world. It is possible to write about power without assuming either that power is an end in itself or that territorial expansion is the chief preoccupation of statesmen. The struggle for power, under those assumptions, could never, even theoretically, come to an end except through successful conquest of the world, and even then the possibility of world-wide civil war could not be excluded. Power in international politics is power *over;* it is a relational concept. It is therefore perfectly obvious that not every state can simultaneously become more powerful. One state's gain is necessarily another's loss, and a loss which the loser will not view with equanimity.

If, however, power is regarded as a means to the attainment of security, the picture need not be quite so black. There are times when nations have refrained from building up their armed forces in particular directions because they would not thereby increase their security. The agreement to keep the long Canadian-American border unfortified must rank as among the major steps in rendering the United States' continental homeland secure. It has permitted the formation of a North American "security union" to the immense advantage of both Canada and the United States.[10] Britain's security has come to depend so largely on America's power (and vice versa) that an improvement in the power position of one no longer induces a sense of insecurity in the other. Americans have not yet made up their minds as to whether the spectacular improvement in the power position of Soviet Russia bodes ill in the long run, although they can hardly be in doubt as to its short-run beneficial effects. For the moment, it is sufficient to point out that the quest for security and the quest for power are not necessarily identical. One state's security is not necessarily every other state's insecurity. Greater security, like greater prosperity but unlike dominant power, is an objective toward which it is at least conceivable that all states can move simultaneously. If "security" is a more accurate word than "domination" to describe the power objectives of leaders of the great states, then there is at least a possibility that in our time the great powers can collaborate in a system of general security. It is only necessary to reiterate that participation in this general security system must seem to offer greater security to *each* of the great powers than nonparticipation.

Which will be the first-rank powers? Are there insuperable barriers to their collaborating with each other? What positive program for collaboration gives greatest promise of a coalition for keeping the peace which will be as effective as the United Nations coalition is for winning the war? Succeeding chapters will deal with these questions.

II. The Custodians of Greatest Power

Adams sought only instruction—wanted only to chart the international channel for fifty years to come; to triangulate the future; to obtain his dimension, and fix the acceleration of movement in politics since the year 1200, as he was trying to fix it in philosophy and physics; in finance and force.
"Education of Henry Adams"

THERE is no mystery about which will be the powers of first rank in the postwar world. The United States of America, Great Britain, and the Soviet Union are the Big Three in war as they will be in peace. However, to understand the significance of this cardinal political fact one must know how they got that way, how their relationships with each other will differ from the relationships of the great powers in the past, and what will be the power position of certain other prominent states which claim great-power status.

Until the twentieth century the great powers were all European powers. Today, none of the three greatest powers is strictly European; nor are any of the three main centers of power located in continental Western Europe. Monopoly in effective use of armed power has certainly passed from the nations of that continent. Today Europe is an arena whose internal struggles periodically involve the whole civilized world in organized bloodshed, and whose struggles end only with the intervention of powers outside the continent. The transition from the old, world-dominating Europe to the new "problem-Europe" is a central fact in the international politics of our time. What are the implications of this outward dispersion of power for the future of Anglo-Soviet-American relations?

The first of the existing world powers was Britain. Her domination of the whole maritime world in the nineteenth century gave her a unique position in relation to the other European powers. Britain's head start in the Industrial Revolution would have guaranteed her a position of primacy in any case.[1] But in an era of water transportation, when overland movement of goods and men was costly and slow, and when the discovery of the New World and the rise of North European trading centers had reoriented Europe toward the Atlantic Ocean, her earlier marginal position became central. She had "the finest site on the Main Street of the world." As an island near the European continent, she could with her mighty navy effectively control the narrow seas through which the men and goods of other powers must pass. Whether by design or by good fortune, acquisition of defensible bases at Gibraltar, Malta, Suez, Aden, Singapore, Capetown, and the Falkland Islands—defensible because they could be supplied most efficiently by the very sea routes whose security their possession ensured—reinforced and perfected the British position. From a communications point of view that country thus controlled both the "main four-corners" of Europe and all its seaward approaches.

In the nineteenth century, however, forces were at work which were to destroy in large part Britain's unique advantages. Her industrial techniques were adopted first across the Atlantic in the United States and then with surprising rapidity in the island empire of Japan.[2]

The United States emerged from its Civil War a nation whose place among the great powers could not long be denied. In terms of its capacity to make war it demonstrated its coming of age by putting into the field in the 1860's armies which were tremendous in size and in striking power. The United States was not for a generation after the Civil War an important naval power, but this was at least partly through choice. Its incomparably bountiful West was a far richer prize than any European power could win by military or naval conquest. That the young giant of the Western Hemisphere was strong enough to repel any European intruder, the ever scheming Napoleon III came to understand after his fiasco in Mexico, when he tried without success to keep the Archduke Maximilian upon the Mexican throne.

Japan, too, experienced large-scale industrialization in the nineteenth century. Although her country lacked rich mineral resources, her statesmen were determined by a total mobilization of her human and mineral resources to make up for this deficiency. Having learned the ways of the Occident, she promptly used her new knowledge to protect herself against the powers of Europe and to assure primacy in the Orient.

With the opening of the twentieth century, therefore, two non-European powers claimed admission to the inner circle of the great powers. By Britain's withdrawal from the Caribbean in the 1890's, symbolized by her reluctant acquiescence in the statement of Secretary of State Olney that "Today the United States is practically sovereign on this continent, and its fiat is law upon the subjects to which it confines its interposition," [3] and by her alliance with Japan in 1902, she acknowledged that the Pax Britannica no longer ran to the ends of the earth. Britain was still the only true world power. She had admitted the regional dominance of the United States and Japan; but without a globe-encircling series of bases these powers were still only regional powers, no matter how big their fleets of capital ships. "Such regional dominance might very well be the most effective means of insuring certain countries—the United States, for example—against blockade or invasion. But . . . no local command of the sea could endow the United States or any other country . . . with a leverage on world politics even approaching that which British statesmen had long derived from their naval ascendancy in Europe's narrow seas."[4] With the formal acceptance of the transoceanic regional powers into the inner circle of the great powers, the first stage in the outward migration of power from Europe was reached.

These moves were certainly hastened by a trend of events within Europe that was equally unfavorable to the maintenance of British maritime supremacy. Brandenburg-Prussia, in the early eighteenth century "Europe's biggest little sand-box," had grown until by 1900 Germany under Kaiser Wilhelm II had won her place as the leading land power of Europe. With the development of the railroad, the strategic position of a centrally located country with an efficient transportation network improved enormously.[5] Bismarck's quick victories against Denmark, Austria, and France gave proof of the new efficiency of overland transport.[6] For Britain this meant a loosening of her former vise-like grip on the main channels of intra-European communication; there were now alternative and speedier routes.

During the mid-nineteenth century, when the Russian bear was the *bête noire* of the British Foreign Office, the further consolidation of North German power under Prussian leadership was watched with friendly interest. But Germany overreached herself. In the words of Sir Eyre Crowe, "Germany had won her place as one of the leading, if not, in fact, the foremost Power on the European continent. But over and beyond the European Great Powers there seemed to stand the 'World Powers.' It was at once clear that Germany must become a 'World Power.'"[7]

This Great Britain was not prepared to admit. Once the German determination to become a world power, by building up a strong fleet, became clear, Britain was necessarily so heavily preoccupied with Europe that her days of unchallenged leadership elsewhere were over. To maintain her physical security at home she was forced to make concessions in America and Asia and to form alliances on the continent of Europe. Her strength after 1900 was still sufficient to make her a valued partner in the alliance system. By forming with France and Russia the Triple Entente the prospects of preserving an equilibrium against the Triple Alliance of the three Central Powers in European politics were somewhat improved, but Britain's days of splendid isolation were over. She was still a power, but only one power in a family of eight. Of these, five were European; two were non-European; and one, Britain, controlled the sea routes between Europe and the outer world.

The First World War saw the complete disintegration of the Austro-Hungarian Empire so that the number of potential candidates for great-power status was permanently reduced by one. Another, Russia, was torn by internal revolution, and, strong or weak, would have been blackballed by the "respectable" powers if her Bolshevik rulers had sought a place for her in the inner circle. A third, Germany, was temporarily so completely disarmed that some of her smaller neighbors, notably Poland, sometimes played a "great-power" role in their relations with her. A fourth, Italy, had at Caporetto and elsewhere made a very poor showing for a power that claimed to be a great power. However, since Italy was on the side of the victors, for the moment no voice was raised to exclude her from the ranks of the powers. With the return of peace there were therefore only four—or, with Italy, five—functioning great powers.

It was the application of the United States' military strength that broke the stalemate in the European War of 1914-18. The United States could no longer, therefore, be classified merely as a regional great power. The second stage in the outward migration of power had now been reached, for a non-European power inclined this balance in Europe as it chose.

The United States had now become in every sense of the word a world power. Her dominant role in the Washington Conference of 1922 showed that she was quite as influential in the Pacific as in Europe. There were, therefore, two world powers after 1919, the United States and Great Britain. The third great power, France, was essentially a European power; and the fourth, Japan, was exclusively an Asiatic power. The first three dominated the Peace Conference of Paris which established the new order in Europe, while the first, second, and fourth dominated the Washington Conference of 1922 which set the pattern of power politics in the Pacific throughout the interwar period.

The twenty-year "long armistice" saw the revival of German power and the re-entry of Russia into the European alliance system. With Italy, which was shortly to reveal its true weakness, there were on the eve of the Second World War seven great powers. The spectacular collapse, first of France and then of Italy, has already reduced the list, for the moment, to five. Few can now doubt that Germany and Japan will also taste the bitter ashes of total defeat. The conclusion of the war will therefore see only three of the original seven still functioning as states of the first rank. The final stage in the outward migration of power from Western Europe will then be reached. No great power will remain in non-Russian continental Europe.

The three survivors—Great Britain, the Soviet Union, and the United States—are all world rather than European powers. The demonstrated military efficiency of the Soviet Union in Europe leaves no doubt that it could give a good account of itself in the Far Eastern conflict zone. It, like Britain and the United States, must be classified as a world power.

The states of continental Western Europe will not, however, be mere pawns in a game of international politics played by outsiders. The rapidity with which De Gaullist France has arisen from the ruins of the Third Republic is a reminder that Europe's political power will be by no means negligible. Complete military defeat is no guarantee against the ultimate reconstruction of the armed force of a defeated state, as the world learned from Germany's spectacular military rebirth in the 1930's. As a member of the winning team, the French National Committee is pressing France's claim for re-entry into the circle of great powers. Germany too will some day reassert its claim to great-power status. Perhaps with less success, so may Italy.

In Asia, there are two candidates for recognition as first-rank powers. China's adherence to the Moscow Declaration and Chiang Kai-shek's participation in a conference at Cairo with Roosevelt and Churchill have been interpreted by many as signifying that the Big Three has already become a Big Four. Since the Japanese will be disinclined to regard their country as a "third-rate power" no matter how complete their defeat in the present war, Japan also will be a candidate.

How many of the five states here mentioned will join the United States, Britain, and the Soviet Union as powers of the first rank after there has been opportunity for recovery from the wounds left by the Second World War? Is a state ever "entitled" to be included in the inner circle? Arguments of a military and of a moral character are frequently intertwined; but one must at the outset distinguish between the "right" to sit in the inner councils of the decision-makers and the "strength" to assume great responsibilities in the postwar world. China, for example, may or may not be accorded "great-power status" in the organization of the peace conference or in some reincarnated League of Nations. Such recognition would not provide a complete answer to the question: "Is China's power now or in the visible future of a magnitude comparable to that of the Soviet Union, the United States, or the British Commonwealth of Nations?" *

After the final Axis defeat, reconstructed France and victorious China will, in their respective spheres of interest, demand a full share in development of the postwar political order. But France is essentially a European and Mediterranean power; even with Indo-China restored she would not really be a great

* For an estimate of China's present and prospective military potential, see the forthcoming volume by David N. Rowe, "China Among the Powers," to be published as a companion volume in the Yale Institute of International Studies series.

power in the Far East. China is exclusively an Asiatic power; no one would expect her to assume responsibilities for the enforcement of security in Europe. Both may be rated as "great" powers in the general international organization which may be set up after the war,* but in contrast with the Big Three, they are only regional powers.

It is not merely the geographically restricted interests of France and China which distinguish them from the Big Three. The artificial character of French hegemony on the continent of Europe in the 1920's was demonstrated by its rapid disintegration during the 1930's. Without support from some or all of the Big Three, her long quest for *sécurité* must remain unsatisfied. Only as a regional partner of the powers with global interests and global resources could she achieve this goal. She will be a valued partner because her European territory could constitute a gigantic bridgehead for military operations against a renewed German aggression, and because her North African territory will in an air age be essential to the maintenance of communications between the Eastern and Western Mediterranean. Her trump card in bidding for support from Great Britain or Russia is the alternative possibility of collaborating very closely with the other. Her chief reliance in demanding help from the Big Three acting in concert will be their interest in preventing her collapse before or her collaboration with a resurgent Germany. France will soon be strong again, but her strength will not be comparable to that of Soviet Russia and the United States and she lacks the far-flung bases of Britain. She will be a power, but a power of declining relative strength in a continent of declining relative strength.

China's position will on the other hand be more favorable

* After Field Marshal Smuts had declared that, as a great power, France was "gone," Major Atlee, as government leader in the House of Commons, found it necessary to quote from the King's speech of November 28, 1943, as follows: "We look forward to the liberation of France and her restoration to the ranks of the Great Powers." *Parliamentary Debates* (Hansard), House of Commons, Vol. 395, No. 7, December 7, 1943, col. 774.

than before the war with respect to her near neighbors. Will she thereby be able to claim full-rank partnership in the post-war aristocracy of world powers? With more than 400,000,000 people in a continental area greater than that of the United States, she possesses two of the necessary qualifications. China, however, is not a power which can undertake great international responsibilities beyond her own borders. She has no armed power available for export. Instead, internal political issues are being decided by external intervention. Chiang Kai-shek's primacy at home depends in large measure on his capacity to attract foreign support. With political and social integration achieved, China will become a most important regional power, but her military might is clearly not of the same order as that of Russia, Britain, or America.

The time and circumstances under which Germany or Japan might be permitted to re-enter the circle of great powers depend on the extent to which the present war coalition coheres in the postwar world; but Germany and Japan too will be at most regional powers, and they may not be powers at all. As for Italy, she should never have been rated as more than the least of the great powers. Her performance in two world wars does not suggest an active role for Italy in the high politics of the postwar world. She has lived like a lion for a day; now she will have to lie down like a lamb for a very long time to come.

There will be no fewer than three and no more than seven great powers. Within this group, there will be "world powers" and "regional powers." These world powers we shall call "super-powers," in order to distinguish them from the other powers which may enjoy the formal and ceremonial prestige of great-power status but whose interests and influence are great in only a single theater of power conflict.* With bases

* In his speech of March 21, 1943, Prime Minister Churchill envisioned as mechanisms for the enforcement of security in the postwar world a "Council of Europe" and a "Council of Asia." Presumably some powers would be a member of both councils, and some others a member of only one. There

both in the East and in the West and with communications assured between East and West, the bulk of the super-powers' armed force is highly mobile. It can, as in the present emergency, be thrown into whichever of the major theaters of war grand strategy dictates.

The three aggregations of power which qualify for status as super-powers on the basis of their world-wide influence would also qualify as super-powers on the basis of military potential greater than that of the other four powers. "Great power plus great mobility of power" describes the super-power. Acting in coalition, the Big Three can bring preponderant power to bear wherever desired. In conflict, they would confront each other on many and widely scattered fronts.

The distribution of armed power in the new world of the super-powers will vary in another significant respect from that of the past. The major centers of industrial power will be widely separated from each other and peripheral with respect to both the European and the East Asian conflict zones. This contrasts with the situation prevailing when a majority of the powers of first rank were located within continental Europe. Especially after the development of the European railway network between 1850 and 1870, high-speed mobilization of land armies made *blitzkrieg* against an adjoining great power practicable.[8] Contrary to popular conception, the true day of the *blitzkrieg* was in the Europe of the 1860's and 1870's, and its day was over long before the first airplane had successfully taken to the air. By the time of the First World War, it had become impossible for a European land power to force a quick decision against a coalition which depended upon arsenals across the water for reinforcements in personnel and matériel. The day of the peripheral super-powers had dawned.

would thus be a differentiation among the great powers similar to that suggested here. The role of the United States in supporting the postwar order might have been made clearer if the two councils had been called the "Council of the West" and the "Council of the East."

The statesmen of the super-powers must remember, however, that military power, like hydroelectric power, can be transmitted to distant points only with much diminished efficiency. The grossly inadequate force with which General MacArthur had to conduct war in the Southwest Pacific in 1942 and 1943 is evidence in point. The gigantic convoys which had to be organized to support the Anglo-American campaign in the Mediterranean and the comparatively small number of front-line divisions which this tremendous effort supported are further proof. Completely adequate communications and supply lines require a substantial diversion of men and matériel from the fighting front. The tanker which carries oil, itself burns oil. The troopship has a permanent crew which will never be part of an invading land force. The steel in the freighter's hull and superstructure will never be available for tanks and guns. The longer the supply line the smaller the proportion of the total military effort which can be applied in actual combat. It is clear therefore that, since the centers of greatest power are more widely separated than heretofore, the new military situation makes it enormously difficult for one super-power to defeat another. Wars between the powers of first rank will necessarily be protracted, far-flung, and indecisive. All ought therefore to be anxious to avoid such a conflict.

Under the old system the proximity of the powers to each other heightened the tension under which the European state system operated. Demands of one great power upon another or upon some small power could not be accepted or rejected by reference to some generally accepted standard called "justice." Since relatively small variations in military power could spell victory or defeat in a war whose imminence it was difficult to judge, concessions were rarely made simply because they were just. In the new situation, on the other hand, relatively small variations in military power will not jeopardize the military security of any of the super-powers. The possibility of settling disputes by compromise or by reference to the merits of the dispute ought correspondingly to be enlarged.

The prospects for a stable and just peace would, therefore, on the basis of this very brief sketch of the world of the super-powers seem to be somewhat improved. A word of warning needs to be injected at this point. The initiative in world politics will have passed from non-Russian continental Europe only if the super-powers recognize that the settlement of Europe is a problem to whose solution they each must contribute. The First World War and the peace conference which followed it were greatly influenced by powers outside Western Europe. The settlement which in 1919 was imposed upon Europe was based upon the assumption that the powers from outside Europe which helped make the peace would also enforce it. In actual fact, in the period between the two world wars, the Western European powers were left largely to their own devices. The centers of great power outside Western Europe all failed to play a constructive role in the maintenance of a stable peace. America's abrupt withdrawal from participation in European affairs, Soviet Russia's ideological intervention in Europe, and Japan's program of imperial expansion were all unsettling factors.[9]

With the outbreak of the Second World War and its subsequent spread from Europe to the rest of the world, Western Europe's incapacity to solve its own problems peacefully was made manifest. The stake of the three peripheral powers in the settlement of Europe was revealed with their own involvement in the war. Unless these three each accept a share of responsibility for the maintenance of stability and peace in Europe after the Second World War, they may expect to become involved in still a third war, world-wide in scope but European in origin.*

* Walter Lippmann in his *U. S. Foreign Policy: Shield of the Republic*, Boston, Little, Brown, 1943, has concluded that the best hope for general peace lies in the organization of security around a nucleus of tripartite co-

The super-powers will also have heavy responsibilities in other zones of conflict in which only their combined influence can preserve stability. Positive collaboration for the stabilizing of Western Europe and Eastern Asia must rest on the interest of each in such a stabilization. It must also rest on the elimination of any conflicts among themselves which might inhibit full co-operation. The possibilities of conflict and co-operation between Britain and America, and between the two great Western democracies and the Soviet Union, will be surveyed before the discussion returns to the formulation of a positive program for maintaining general security in the postwar world.

operation. Carl Becker in his *How New Will the Better World Be?*, New York, Knopf, 1944, supports this view and believes that the prospects for collaboration between the Western powers and the Soviet Union are quite good.

… *PART TWO*

BRITAIN AND AMERICA

III. Britain vs. America

> *With infinite effort he [Hay] had achieved the astonishing diplomatic feat of inducing the Senate, with only six negative votes, to permit Great Britain to renounce, without equivalent, treaty rights which she had for fifty years defended tooth and nail.*
> "Education of Henry Adams"

CONFLICTS between Great Britain and the United States have not in this century been settled by men who envisioned an ultimate resort to war. Either power may therefore, in its dealings with third states, safely leave its flanks exposed to the other. This is the basic fact which permits Britain and America to contemplate without alarm improvements in each other's power position and which makes it rational that each should explore fully the possibilities of political collaboration with the other.

It has not always been thus. For a generation after the American Revolution disputes growing out of the political separation embroiled their relations and culminated finally in the War of 1812.[1] One such dispute, that over fishing rights off the coasts of Newfoundland, was not finally settled until the twentieth century.

A second major source of Anglo-American dispute is only in our own day beginning to lose its importance. Until the United States had itself developed a powerful navy, its commerce on the high seas was better protected by international law than by fleet action. This of course brought the United States, in an era such as that between 1815 and 1914 when wars were short and localized, into only intermittent conflict with the British mistress of the seas, for whom every expansion of neutral rights was a limitation on her own freedom of action. With both Britain and America now possessing great navies and with Anglo-American agreement on the necessity for using force to restrain aggressors, the extent of neutral rights will not be an issue between them in the event of renewed general war.

A third type of dispute disappeared with British recognition in the 1890's of the paramount position of the United States in this hemisphere. The classic statement of United States primacy in this hemisphere, the Monroe Doctrine, did not establish the paramount American position *vis-à-vis* Great Britain. It was Britain's naval supremacy much more than James Monroe's pronouncement which kept the continental European powers from intervening in New World affairs in 1823; Canning's famous memorandum to the French ambassador, Polignac, on October 9, 1823, nearly two months before Monroe's statement of December 2, 1823, stated Britain's determination to keep the rest of Europe out of Latin America.[2]

Had the United States been powerful enough at the time to jeopardize Britain's interests in the New World, Canning might have made it equally clear that Britain was determined to keep the United States out too. One of Canning's most devoted followers asserted in the House of Commons in 1830 that Britain could never permit the United States to expand in the Caribbean or establish maritime supremacy in the New World. In this connection Alfred Vagts has written: "America, the international order of things in the Americas, for nearly a century after the Peace of Ghent lived in the umbrella shade of the old mistress of the seas who luckily for these ungracious protégés was not also a land power or military power. . . ."[3]

By the end of the nineteenth century, Britain's position in the Americas and the world had altered. Its more vulnerable position in Europe made that power anxious to avoid strife in the rest of the world and indeed to forge alliances with the new extra-European powers.* Britain was not a land power and could not in any case have prevented the development of the United States as a continental power. Since an independent and efficiently governed United States provided the same opportunity for British investment in the New World that a reconquered United States would have and at less cost, she may have been less anxious to check the rising American power. Finally, democratic elements in the English body politic would have turned out a government which pursued a purely Machiavellian policy toward their transatlantic cousins. For some or all of these reasons, problems arising out of the United States' determination to establish a paramount position in the New World suddenly ceased to be problems. Anglo-American relations were therefore redefined between 1895 and 1905 on the basis of British recognition of the American position.[4]

What is significant for the student of contemporary power politics is that a final Anglo-American war proved unnecessary to establish this dominance.[5] At least until the present war the Communists have been unable to grasp the fact that the moment for Anglo-American war passed nearly fifty years ago. In 1928 Joseph Stalin spoke of "the struggle for world hegemony ... between England, whose star is setting, and America, whose star is in the ascendant." He said: "What does this fundamental antagonism augur? It most undoubtedly augurs war."[6]

During the period between the Venezuelan boundary dispute in 1895 and the final delineation of the Alaskan Panhandle boundary in the so-called arbitration of 1903, the United States pursued a "kill-or-cure" diplomacy which fortunately turned out to be a cure. Lord Salisbury's final, reluctant agreement to arbitration of the Venezuelan dispute after Secretary of State

---

* Cf. *supra*, pp. 13-16.

Olney's bald assertion of American supremacy * was the signal for general retreat in New World politics. Not since that day has any responsible American in public life called for war with Britain.†

The withdrawal of the British Caribbean squadron to waters nearer home, the dismantling of fortifications in the Caribbean and in Canada, the renegotiation of the Isthmian Canal question to permit the United States to build and operate the Panama Canal alone, and finally the sacrifice of the Canadian claim in the Alaskan boundary dispute, all were evidences of British retreat. Henceforth, the way was open for Anglo-American collaboration, especially since the United States did not challenge British interests in Europe or other parts of the world.

In the relations between two democratically organized states, however, positive co-operation must rest upon a broader basis than mere absence of insoluble disputes. "Phobias," if entertained by numerically important or strategically placed minorities in one country, may inhibit active collaboration with the other. So may the many minor disputes which with good will on both sides could be eliminated. Finally, since co-operative policy must be based upon a widespread public belief that the moral and strategic foundations for joint action exist, there must be public discussion of the opportunities for positive col-

* Quoted *supra*, p. 14.

† In 1895, on the other hand, Theodore Roosevelt was writing Henry Cabot Lodge: "Personally I rather hope the fight will come soon. The clamor of the peace faction has convinced me that this country needs a war." Henry C. Lodge, ed., *Selections from the Correspondence of Theodore Roosevelt and Henry Cabot Lodge*, New York, Scribners, 1925, Vol. I, pp. 204-05. Even Woodrow Wilson supported the forthright stand of President Cleveland and Secretary Olney. By way of contrast, in England, Arthur Balfour said at this time that the idea of war with the United States struck him with "some of the unnatural horror of a civil war." Blanche Dugdale, *Arthur James Balfour*, New York, Putnam, 1937, Vol. I, p. 226, cited by Lionel Gelber, *The Rise of Anglo-American Friendship*, New York, Oxford University Press, 1938, p. 19.

laboration. The remainder of this chapter will therefore deal with divisive attitudes, conflicts, and misunderstandings which are either unnecessary or minor, and with opportunities for indirect contribution to the security problem through co-operation. The next will discuss the moral and material bases of common policy.

With American entry into the First World War, enthusiasm in Britain for all things American knew no bounds. Its only parallel was the sudden rise to popularity in Britain of Soviet Russia in 1941, when the Red Army so unexpectedly saved British cities from a continued air bombardment and Britain itself from the possibility of invasion. The United States' abrupt withdrawal from European politics after 1919 was a rude shock to the expectations of the masses of the people. As a consequence, the average Englishman today may be more skeptical of the possibilities of Anglo-American collaboration than he is hostile to the idea. There is a widespread feeling that, with the peace-time primacy of domestic over foreign affairs in the United States, the latter country cannot be depended upon to fulfill international commitments made in a war emergency.

For a number of reasons unfriendly attitudes in the United States toward Great Britain are more of an obstacle to collaboration than are unfriendly attitudes in Britain toward America. There are, for example, no groups in Britain such as the Daughters of the American Revolution which makes a cult of the tradition of heroic resistance against the English. Britain, after all, never had to fight for freedom from America. She had other traditional enemies. Also, her constitutional system does not require that lengthy debates precede the ratification of each treaty. This reduces the danger that demagogic appeals might stimulate or inflame mass prejudices. Finally, the British electoral system does not heighten the importance of some strategically located minority such as the Irish-Americans of Brooklyn or Boston.

The advocate of closer Anglo-American co-operation in the

United States has a difficult, though perhaps in recent years decreasingly difficult, task. One difficulty was the belief that, if a policy coincided with British policy, it involved truckling to the Union Jack. The result has been in certain periods of our history, notably 1875-1900, a "truckling to the Shamrock." [7] In successive presidential elections in that period, the final outcome was so close that the electoral votes of New York determined the result. Within the State of New York, the two major parties were so evenly divided that the "hyphenated Americans" and especially the Irish-American voters of New York City had a political influence out of all proportion to their numbers, which were in any case not small.

That part of the American people originally of British origin came to this country at an earlier period. Their descendants are therefore more completely assimilated and are "American" rather than "British-American." With the partial exception of the upper middle-class, suburban, Eastern-seaboard groups there are no concentrations of vigorous pro-British groups. For the rest, Anglophile sentiment is widely diffused and therefore politically less effective than Anglophobe sentiment.

With the cessation of mass immigration to the United States after 1921, there has been a notable "dehyphenization" of the American stock of non-British origin. The neutrality of Eire in the present war may serve further to drive a wedge between the Irish of Eire and Americans of Irish descent whose sons are fighting for the United States.

The expression of anti-British sentiments in America still, however, strikes a tremendously responsive chord. On the eve of the present war, it was still fashionable to say that the United States had entered the First World War to save the $500,000,000 which J. P. Morgan had granted the government of Great Britain for purchases of war materials in this country.[8] Mr. Quincy Howe in two books, *England Expects Every American to Do His Duty* and *Blood Is Cheaper than Water*,[9] popularized the idea that Americans had been and were in danger of continuing to be dupes of the wily British diplomats. The traditionally Anglophobe press has during the war hidden its peace-time bias under the cloak of advocacy of a "Pacific First" strategy and, by implication, of a substantial diversion of the American military effort from the European war.*

The still widely prevalent, even though lessening, Anglophobia in the United States feeds on minor disputes and false rumors. If Anglo-American collaboration is viewed as essential to American security, it is important to identify, with a view to their elimination as promptly as possible, minor disputes which are susceptible of solution, and rumors and beliefs which are the carriers of Anglophobe propaganda. Otherwise it may not be possible fully to harvest the fruits of common victory.

Some especially troublesome sources of friction that must be dealt with may be listed to indicate the gravity of the problem. Those listed below are to be regarded as typical; the list makes no pretense to completeness. The most troublesome are those in which one's gain is apparently the other's loss, e.g.:

(1) Postwar United States dependence on the rubber and tin of Southeast Asia. Formerly a prolific source of dollar exchange for the British and Netherlands empires, this area may become just another imperial slum and the colonial powers administering the area may find their pattern of international trade seriously dislocated if the United States decides not again to become dependent on the area for strategic raw materials.†

---

* Colonel Robert R. McCormick, publisher of the Chicago *Tribune*, no longer feels it necessary to mask his Anglophobia with a "Pacific First" program. His "revelation" on December 16, 1943, that he helped save Detroit from British invasion in 1921 can hardly have been calculated to promote Anglo-American unity in the war and after. Chicago *Tribune*, December 16, 1943, pp. 1, 6.

† If there is a genuine desire on both sides to discover an equitable solution, this source of conflict, like so many others, can be eliminated. By a combination of stock-piling natural rubber, of subsidizing the production of some artificial rubber, and of maintaining "shadow" factories so as to permit the rapid resumption in a new crisis of full-scale artificial rubber production,

(2) British investments in Latin America. From the British point of view, inter-American solidarity ought not to be purchased at the expense of the creditor, including the British creditor. This apparently occurred in the case of the Mexican oil expropriations. The basic difficulty is probably that the United States can afford better than Britain to purchase the good will of its "good neighbors" to the South by failing to support strongly its own nationals' creditor and proprietor interests.

(3) Surplus shipping and shipbuilding capacity. The enormous expansion of the American merchant marine during the war will not be followed by an equally drastic contraction. To the British, on the other hand, with their creditor position destroyed, it will be more than ever important to have a large share of the world's carrying trade. Resentment will be especially acute in Great Britain if the United States' enlarged share in postwar shipping is preserved with the aid of a subsidy so huge that neither the British nor the Americans can make any money in the shipping field.

(4) Conflicting trade policies. With the almost complete liquidation of British foreign investments abroad, with decreasing American reliance on the rubber and tin of the Malayan peninsula, and with the United States the possessor of a large merchant marine which will carry goods formerly transported in British bottoms, three former sources of dollar exchange will be almost eliminated. British trade policy is therefore likely to be based upon state control of the direction of foreign trade in order to increase the trade within the sterling bloc. American policy, on the other hand, has avowedly been directed toward the unclogging of the channels of international trade, toward the elimination of exchange control, and toward equality of treatment for all trading nations.

the United States could with safety resume systematic purchase of Malayan rubber. See K. E. Knorr, *Rubber after the War*, Food Research Institute, Stanford University, 1944.

(5) Transoceanic commercial aviation. The superior productive facilities of the United States and the more widespread distribution of landing rights in the hands of the British might seem to furnish the basis for a compromise. However, American concentration on the building of four-motor bombers and cargo transport planes during the war and Pan-American Airways' near monopoly of transoceanic private air enterprise, secured at a time when the personnel and equipment of its British competitors were being diverted to a more direct war use, may make Britain sensitive to any "unfair" attempts by American private enterprise to retain advantages which were a by-product of a common war effort. Americans, on the other hand, will be quick to resent the exclusion of American commercial aviation enterprise from airfields built all over the world with lend-lease funds.

(6) Markets in semicolonial areas. Especially in Latin America but perhaps also in China and Central Europe, postwar Britain would find it difficult to recapture her prewar position in raw material-producing countries in the face of cheap American credit extended for political rather than economic reasons.

(7) Surplus grain production. The politically important farm bloc in the United States may be determined to export wheat no matter what government subsidy may be required or what countervailing duties against wheat dumped abroad may be levied in foreign countries. Great Britain will certainly not be opposed in principle to receiving at an artificially low price the grain which she desperately needs from abroad. However, it is cheap grain from the Dominions rather than merely cheap grain which she desires. An American grain export subsidy which destroyed the possibility of Dominion profit in wheat-growing would be highly objectionable.

(8) Palestine and the Arab world. Many Americans, especially many of Jewish extraction, are interested in the fulfillment of the Balfour commitment to create a Jewish national

homeland in Palestine. Great Britain, with the integrity of its Empire threatened by unfriendly elements in the Arab world, is pursuing a policy which is cautious with respect to the Arabs and irritating to large elements in America. Public attention is more and more being focused on the huge oil reserves of the Arabian peninsula. They have lent new importance to any divergence of policy over the Arabs.

None of these sources of friction can be described as a fundamental conflict of interest although, together with many other similar potential disputes, they can in the aggregate be a potent cause of non-co-operation. Where influential private interests are involved, settlement will be difficult. If, however, there is joint recognition of a higher interest in security and stability, then fair play, compromise, and foresight can lessen the impact of clashing private groups sufficiently to permit collaboration in problems of security.

Actual disputes can always be the subject of negotiation, and there thus exists the possibility of their elimination by agreement. More difficult to eliminate and, in the relations between democracies, probably more effective in paralyzing the will to collaborate are resentments, suspicions, and doubts about the other country's motives or its reliability in the hour of crisis. Even during the present conflagration doubts about the purity of other members of the bucket brigade have sometimes lessened the zeal for fire-fighting. Unless these doubts are stilled, the effectiveness of co-operation to prevent a new fire from breaking out will be jeopardized. A representative but not complete list of barriers to Anglo-American understanding may be mentioned.

(1) India. The powerful influence of the ascetic Mahatma Gandhi on "right-minded" American and British opinion has greatly complicated Anglo-Indian relations. Americans suspect that Great Britain is procrastinating over the question of Indian independence in order to hold on a little longer to the spoils of Empire. For the future of Anglo-American relations, this sus-

picion may be more important than the future of the Indian question itself.

(2) "Empire." This important symbol has a favorable connotation in England and a wholly evil connotation in America. Winston Churchill's oft-quoted statement that he had not been called to be the King's first minister in order to preside over the liquidation of the British Empire made a painful impression in the United States. To the Anglophobe, it was as if a nation which the United States had rescued on the promise to "go straight" had slipped back into unrepentant "imperialism."

(3) "Blood" versus "dollars." Any attempt to secure substantial repayment to the United States of funds advanced under the lend-lease program will reactivate the old First World War controversy as to whether British blood or American dollars won the war. Even more dangerous will be an attempt to link up cancellation of debts created under lend-lease with political or trade concessions. Lend-lease was originally associated in the public mind with "aid to Britain." The valid reason for aiding Britain, that she was fighting America's fight and that therefore aid to Britain was in fact aid to the United States since it gave America the time to rearm, has often been forgotten.*

(4) Reciprocally bad stereotypes of each other's diplomacy. John Bull is always shown as the "slick" diplomat to whom our gullible Uncle Sam owes his downfall. To the British, our diplomacy appears meddlesome, reactionary, and unreliable, while their own—except for the painful Baldwin-Chamberlain interlude—they think of as "steadfast." The sharp contrast, for example, in the 'thirties between Secretary Hull's apparent readiness to fulminate against the totalitarian aggressor and lawbreaker, and his hesitation in committing the United States

* It would be as logical to charge the United States for the training, upkeep, and pay of the British soldiers firing American-made munitions at the common enemy as to charge Great Britain for the American bullets expended in a joint cause.

to use force under any circumstances, illustrates the "meddlesome" aspect.[10] Our rapid and precipitate withdrawal from European politics after the First World War is responsible for our reputation for unreliability. Each nation suspects the diplomats of the other of hypocrisy.

(5) Divergent internal political programs. It is whispered in some quarters that a leftward drift of British politics would mean a pro-Russian, and therefore by implication *not* pro-American, orientation in British policy. Many Englishmen, on the other hand, believe that the United States is on the verge of a conservative reaction. Since they associate Republicanism and isolationism, they expect a new period of irresponsible non-participation in world politics.

(6) Disarmament. The British Empire and the United States have in the last decade greatly jeopardized each other's security by a failure to keep armaments up to a level which corresponded to the responsibilities of each for self-defense. The surrender at Munich and the rapid disintegration of the Philippine defenses were disasters for both. Doubters in each country will watch critically for signs of inadequate armaments in the other in the postwar years and may then call for an alternative foreign policy.

(7) Constitutional difficulties—the United States Senate. Kenneth Colegrove recently asserted that "our faulty ratification process may be a menace to world peace as surely as is the *Führer* principle in Nazi Germany, or dual diplomacy in Nippon."[11] This statement may be extreme, but it reflects a widespread belief in other countries that the United States is constitutionally unfitted to assume a role of constructive world leadership and is therefore an undependable partner.

(8) The declining role of Britain in world affairs. Gradually but inevitably Britain is becoming the lesser partner in Anglo-American ventures. This is very unpleasant to many Englishmen who will not be any more friendly to the United States on that account. An especial degree of forbearance and tact on

the part of Americans is necessary to make the transition easy and to permit the United States to benefit fully from the many boons which a friendly and co-operative Britain can still confer upon us.

The various hostile attitudes, conflicts, and sources of irritation here catalogued tend to prevent an objective appraisal of Anglo-American strategic interdependence by both the peoples involved. They also tend to prevent positive co-operation in those fields where co-operation is necessary to provide an atmosphere in which security arrangements have some hope of functioning with success.

Britain and America must assume leadership for the restoration of devastated areas, the conversion of the world's war-torn economy to a peace-time basis, and the development of colonial areas. Although the tasks of reconstruction can find adequate justification either on purely humanitarian grounds or on grounds of economic self-interest, security considerations also dictate Anglo-American collaboration to promote economic well-being throughout the devastated and the backward areas. The essentially economic tasks of relief, rehabilitation, and reconstruction in a sense take primacy over the purely political tasks because Europe cannot wait to take steps to feed and clothe and shelter itself while United Nations statesmen debate. Britain and America must also play a large part in maintaining the security of the new world order against a new aggressor. In the first group of tasks, they will find the good will of Soviet Russia essential, but that country's own tasks of reconstruction will be so enormous that it ought to be a recipient rather than a donor of aid in the rehabilitation and rebuilding of war-torn areas. The apparent preference of Soviet planners for a substantial degree of economic self-sufficiency would also point logically to the assumption by the Anglo-Americans of leadership in the longer-term program for economic reconstruction. On the other hand, those responsibilities more directly related to the enforcement of security cannot properly be discussed in purely Anglo-American terms since the character of the problem will be largely determined by the relations of the Western democracies to the Soviet Union.

British and American acts either of omission or of commission in economic reconstruction will have repercussions on the security problem. It is banal but important to observe that a speedy conversion from a war-time to a peace-time economy is necessary to avoid the popularization of programs of chauvinist expansion and nationalist revolution in postwar Europe. Prolonging the period of conversion exposes the postwar world to the triple dangers of inflation, insecurity, and depression. The impoverished and frustrated salaried classes, the maladjusted veteran incapable of assimilation into civilian society, and the jobless [12] might again seek to relieve their personal anxieties by completely identifying themselves with new militant regimes and by supporting organized aggression. Without a return of moderate prosperity and reasonably full employment Anglo-American leadership would seem to the smaller nations of Europe only less odious than Axis domination.

The task of greatest urgency on the day a given area is liberated will be to rush food and medical supplies to the starving, the sick, and the homeless populations.[13] This will not be done as an act of charity but to meet the legitimate needs of the victims of war for a chance to work out their own problems. The traditional willingness of the United States to provide relief, in the event of famine or disaster, and the evident need of the war-torn areas make it possible that this task can be performed with speed, efficiency, and mutual satisfaction. The extensive planning here under Herbert H. Lehman and in Britain under Sir Frederick Leith-Ross, the creation with forty-four participating nations of the United Nations Relief and Rehabilitation Administration (UNRRA), the detailed and frugal estimates by the governments-in-exile of their respective needs, all testify to an advanced state of readiness to deal with this problem. Almost as urgent will be the tasks of rehabilitation including the provision of seed, fertilizer, and the tools necessary to the functioning of consumers' goods and transport industries.

Even these humanitarian activities have security aspects. In the highly suggestive state of public opinion on the dawn of peace, with the people prepared to follow whichever group promises law, order, food, and a job, the channels through which relief is to be distributed must be selected with great care. The choice may have, in the domestic politics of the country concerned, long-range political consequences. It may also have important consequences for the emerging pattern of power politics. Soviet leaders will watch with unflagging attention for signs that the Western donors of relief are encouraging the formation of anti-Soviet or anti-Communist governments by granting or withholding food on some other basis than needs or by selecting the channels for distributing it. The Russian communists have, of course, charged Herbert Hoover's relief program after the First World War with having been in Russia and Eastern Europe an instrument of "White" reaction.*

* "It was Hoover's idea that when the people of Russia should be faced with the alternative: Biscuits or Bolshevism, they would undoubtedly choose Biscuits. But the Russian people soon found that the Biscuits had a very important string tied to them. That string was Reaction, and the complete restoration of the old régime." *Soviet Russia*, October 11, 1919, p. 20. "Experience has proved that whenever the Allies really want some of their lesser brethren to pursue a certain policy, they do not even have to employ military measures to gain their end. They control the food situation of the world." *Ibid.*, August 16, 1919, p. 10.

Woodrow Wilson's own recognition of the political implications of food relief is shown by the following communication to his secretary in Washington in support of Herbert Hoover's request for funds for this purpose, as follows: "Tumulty, The White House, Washington. Please convey following confidential message to Senator Martin and Congressman Swager Sherley: 'I can not too earnestly or solemnly urge upon the Congress the appropriation for which Mr. Hoover has asked for the administration of food relief. Food relief is now the key to the whole European situation and to the solution of peace. Bolshevism is steadily advancing westward, has overwhelmed Poland, and is poisoning Germany. It can not be stopped by force. . . . The money . . . will be spent for financing the movement of

In measures relating to the revival of international trading an Anglo-American agreement would in all probability be one to which the smaller states of Europe might subscribe, for the British foreign trade position will be so similar to that of much of continental Europe that she will perforce represent its interests. With the almost complete liquidation of British and continental foreign investments, remittances from abroad will be small. Imports can only be kept up by more exports, and for Britain and Europe alike only more exports will permit a return even to a prewar standard of living.

America must recognize that her own security, even more than her prosperity, demands economic revival in Europe. If the trade policies of Secretary Hull are not continued, if no way is found to revive international trading, it may, for the United States, in the first instance be only expensive. For others, it will be disastrous. Fomenting economic catastrophe abroad furnishes a poor basis either for American or for British-American leadership in the restoration of European political stability.

Still another security aspect of the problem of trade revival in Europe is the necessity of keeping Norway, Holland, Belgium, and the agricultural Balkans from being too dependent on the German market for their products. The first three countries have in the past extensively engaged in transoceanic rather than strictly intra-European trading and will want to do so again. Agricultural Eastern Europe has in the last decade learned how too great dependence on a single customer, Germany, can lead to political dependence. Opening the American and British Empire markets to the products of Europe can, therefore, deprive Germany of a powerful weapon in the event of a new attempt at European hegemony.

food to our real friends in Poland and to the people of the liberated units of the Austro-Hungarian Empire, and to our associates in the Balkans. . . .' Woodrow Wilson." *Congressional Record*, January 20, 1919, Vol. 57, Pt. 2, p. 1753.

The rebuilding of heavy industry and the program of long-term reconstruction generally will require large credits which, whatever the mechanism for allocation, must in the main come from the United States. Here, too, it is necessary for the governments of Great Britain and the United States to act with great care lest their ultimate objective seem to the Soviet government to be the creation of puppet regimes which would one day be satellites of an anti-Soviet coalition.*

The problems of the colonial world in the Caribbean, in Africa below the Sahara, and in Southeast Asia and Indonesia must also be solved under Anglo-American leadership.† Not only the continued existence of the British Empire but also that of the Belgian and Dutch Empires depends upon Anglo-American victory and future control by Britain and America of the sea routes of the world.

To nations which style themselves "freedom-loving" the interests of the colonial people themselves could not in any case be a matter of indifference, but self-interest demands that these areas not again be permitted to become breeders of suspicion among the powers. Charges of economic exploitation on one side and of ideological exploitation on the other lead to increasing bitterness.‡ The colonial powers, as well as the United States, which has committed itself to the maintenance at least until after this war of the territorial integrity of the colonial

---

* Cf. *infra*, pp. 120, 126-27.

† French North Africa and the Near East are properly treated as parts of the European power zone. The tiny islets of the Pacific and the strong points commanding narrow seas, both of which have numerically small native populations, raise strategic rather than colonial problems. These areas are accordingly excluded from the discussion of colonial areas which follows.

‡ The establishment of the Anglo-American Caribbean Commission shows the determination of Britain and America to cope with the problem. Although the Caribbean colonies of the two powers present fewer strategic problems than do the colonies of Malaysia and their small size precludes complete independence as a satisfactory ultimate solution, the work of this Commission may be of very great value in developing a colonial policy capable of general application.

empires, must give convincing proof to the world of a new sense of responsibility.

Especially in their relations with the Soviet Union is this demonstration of disinterestedness a matter of practical politics. That power has under its tutelage in its Asiatic hinterland many backward peoples, but it has never been and is not now a participant in the scramble for colonial territory in Africa or Southeast Asia. On the other hand, the slogans of "liberation nationalism," which, by the U.S.S.R. Constitution of 1936 and by earlier Soviet policy, were officially encouraged, will continue to agitate the colonial peoples. Thus, from the point of view of Soviet relations the task of the Western democracies is to develop colonial policies calculated to weaken the disruptive appeal which these slogans make to native populations.

The obvious, if not wholly adequate, answer, one which would be a complete demonstration of disinterestedness, would be to grant the various colonial areas independence as rapidly as elements within the colonial population become vocal in the demand for it. In the present era, in which the colonial powers find themselves saddled with a herculean task of equatorial slum clearance, the colonies may possibly find that independence is as attractive a solution for the mother country as it is for the colonial elite which would take over in the event of complete self-government. An alternative course of action, which would also give convincing evidence of disinterestedness, would be to turn over the administration of colonial areas to presumably impartial international agencies operating in the name of the civilized world community. Except for League of Nations experience in supervising the government of the Saar for fifteen years, there is little precedent for such an arrangement. A third solution would be continued national administration but with strict accountability to international agencies of supervision and inspection. Still a fourth solution would be an "equitable" division of colonial areas between the present colonial powers and those noncolonial powers which assert that they are fitted and entitled and willing to undertake responsibility for colonial administration. Such a solution would involve a cynical disregard for native interests and need not be discussed further.

Whatever solution is adopted, the responsibilities to the local population of the administering power would appear to be three. (1) It must avoid the creation of a strategic vacuum in the area, a matter which will be discussed in greater detail later. This means that, from the colonial people's point of view, it must provide external protection. Guaranteeing protection is not a purely military matter since policy must be designed to eliminate the feeling of discrimination by noncolonial powers. (2) It must provide, at a reasonable price, the "know-how," wherever native skills are unavailable, to assure the performance of essential police, economic, and social service functions. (3) Finally, it must actively foster policies by which, without endangering local minorities or inducing economic decline or creating a strategic vacuum, the share of the local leadership in the partnership of colonial administration will be constantly enlarged.

Those who advocate complete and early independence as a solution for many colonial areas frequently make comparisons unfavorable to the British between our policy in the Philippines and theirs in India. We have scheduled independence for the Philippines at a fixed date which we are apparently prepared to move forward. They have scheduled independence for India "after the war" and continue to stress British responsibility for the large Moslem minorities whose interests would presumably be threatened by British withdrawal. Neither power has yet shown how independence can be granted under conditions which guarantee solution of the long-range problems of economic development and military security. In both cases, and elsewhere throughout the colonial world, the improved efficiency of public services, especially in the field of public health, have permitted a gigantic population increase—perhaps, in the case of India, of fifty million in the last decade—to a point at which neither a decent minimum standard of living nor an effective military defense is possible. The mere grant of independence will not solve but might well intensify these problems. Except for a very few of the more advanced and more populous colonies such as Ceylon, the grant of independence at the present stage of their development would be irresponsible. No adequate provision could be made for the fulfillment of any of the three types of obligation regarding security, welfare, and orderly autonomous development. For the present discussion, it is enough to stress the importance of not creating a strategic vacuum.

As for administration by some international agency, it is easier to see why that administration might be disinterested than why it would be efficient. It would, in the beginning at least, lack a colonial civil service with smoothly functioning techniques of government and in all probability would be incapable of acting with vigor. In a world of power politics it would lack the means of defending its colonial responsibilities. Continued national administration but with effective international agencies of supervision and inspection would seem to achieve the objectives of supra-national administration without the attendant disadvantages. It would combine the advantages of vigorous and single-headed administration with fixed responsibility by a power with trained colonial civil servants and third-party disinterested judgment on the fairness and effectiveness of this administration.

There is one danger to which Anglo-American leadership is exposed in its dealings with the colonial populations. The "White Australia" policy; the American practice of "Oriental exclusion"; * racial segregation in the upper-class social life of Singapore, Calcutta, Manila, and the British and American colonies generally; the ostentatious precautions of the British

* By recent legislation the immigration of Chinese to the United States is to be restricted by a method much less offensive to the Chinese people. 78th Congress, First Session, Public Law No. 199.

colonial civil servant against "going native"; the unsavory American reputation for the treatment of Negroes in the Southern states—all these furnish the basis for a powerful propaganda which could negate the effects of Anglo-American policy, however benevolent or well-intentioned. The slightest exhibition of arrogant superiority feeds the flames of anti-white passion not only among the colonial peoples but among the independent peoples of Asia. The race aspect of the colonial problem is almost more important in its effect on British and American relations with China, and perhaps with India, than it is in the colonies themselves. The Japanese have temporarily tarnished the "Asia for the Asiatics" slogan, but it could easily be the rallying cry for a new war which would take the form of a great inter-racial struggle between the yellow and brown East and the white West.

From the point of view of British and American relations with the European noncolonial powers, the task is to develop colonial economic policies sufficiently liberal to deny the "have-not" powers a plausible case for aggression. This latter group of powers has complained that it has had to pay tribute because of the monopoly prices charged for products coming from colonies containing artificially scarce raw materials. Equitable exploitation by the imperial overlords is essential to reduce the competition for imperial expansion based on the belief that "colonies pay." In urging moderation on these powers the United States, because of its prewar dependence on the products of Malaya and Indonesia, may be expected to range itself on the side of the smaller noncolonial powers.

Anglo-American domination of the sea routes between raw material-producing and industrial areas should not, in an era of liberal colonial trading policies, be a threat to any power except in the event of war. If one assumes a widespread belief among the smaller nations that the English-speaking powers will not be the aggressors, then the small-power non-aggressors will have little reason to organize against Anglo-American control of the seas. Objections to Anglo-American naval dominance by powers which plan to acquire colonies by force would of course have no standing. Such objections would instead lend point to the important security function which the English-speaking powers assert that they still have to perform in colonial areas. The colonies, like the League of Nations mandates, would be described by them as areas "which are inhabited by peoples not yet able to stand by themselves under the strenuous conditions of the modern world."

The course of Japan's southward advance demonstrates the importance of the Malayan and Indonesian colonial area as a zone of conflict. Its rubber and tin are of first-rate importance to Britain and America. So is the denial to Japan of its petroleum. Military responsibilities are in fact likely to persist long after economic opportunity has vanished, for the strategic vacuum created by Anglo-American withdrawal would be more of a threat to powers with a vested interest in peace and stability than to those with aggressive and expansionist designs. The Philippine Islands, for example, may be the "strategic liability" which many have called them, but they cannot on that account be simply "written off." For both Britain and America the inescapable responsibility will probably be greater than the privilege; and there is, therefore, every incentive to share the burden, especially with each other.*

Are there insurmountable barriers to Anglo-American collaboration? The greatest barrier of all, war, is in the case of these two powers an obstacle of slight importance. The choice,

* In terms of practical policy this conclusion would support the present grand strategy of the war. By postponing the final showdown with Japan until both powers are in a position to act, the end of the war will see the military position of both reconstituted. A sharing of responsibility for stability would then be possible. A purely American campaign in support of China and against Japan, favored by advocates of a "Pacific First" strategy, would have permitted a wedge to be driven between the British and American positions in Southeast Asia and thus have further unsettled the political equilibrium of the region.

therefore, with respect to common Anglo-American objectives is between an ineffective working at cross purposes and an effective co-ordination of policy. The matters actually or potentially in dispute are exacerbated by a variety of resentments and hostile attitudes, especially in the United States. They do tend to inhibit co-operative action except in grave crises, but as disputes they cannot be described as fundamental. They should not be permitted to hamstring policy based on the fundamental interdependence of Britain and America on each other for security in a very insecure world. It would, therefore, be a substantial if indirect contribution to joint security if "minor" disputes could be settled and mutual doubts allayed. This would pave the way for the program of positive co-operation in European reconstruction and in colonial development and thus create an environment in which a security program could function with an optimum chance of success.

IV. Strategic Interdependence

*For what we are about to eat
Let's thank the Lord and the British Fleet.*
New Zealand High Commissioner in
London, improvising thanks for a meal.

EFFORTS to place Anglo-American collaboration on the unsentimental basis of an identity of strategic interest have sometimes underemphasized the nonmaterial factors which permit each nation to contemplate threats to its own security in terms which exclude the other as a possible enemy. In writing of the Anglo-American partnership in the First World War, Forrest Davis declares that the joint aim was "command of the Atlantic." The enemy, he writes, "happened to be a dynastic, militarized state, an 'autocracy'; . . . our aim would have been the same had the enemy been a republic or a constitutional monarchy."[1] The implication, although it is not directly stated, is that "our aim would have been the same had our ally been a dynastic, militarized state, an 'autocracy.'" "Command of the Atlantic," secured only by tremendous and co-ordinated Anglo-American effort, has been important to both countries because it permitted a pooling of the military strength of two powerful nations, each of which regarded the other as a reliable ally. The ally's reliability was not wholly due to its geographic position, but also in part to its democratic social organization.

In both countries, there is a belief in the dignity and value of the individual and a disbelief in the state as an end in itself.

Steps in foreign policy are tested by such considerations of security as: "Will our homes and our way of life be threatened by a failure to take this step?" Public opinion has not always answered such a question correctly, and incorrect answers have sometimes resulted in extremely maladroit policies being pursued. This mode of thinking about foreign affairs, however, has certainly made the people of each of the two countries less sensitive to improvements in the power position of the other.

In neither country is there a substantial percentage of people who covet additional territory for their state simply in order to add to the state's reputation for power. Still smaller is the group which covets territory now held by the other.[2] Senator Chandler of Kentucky has spoken for American retention of certain islets in the Pacific over which Great Britain is now the legal sovereign in partial payment for lend-lease aid.[3] The anti-British character of his previous speeches deprived this speech of whatever newsworthy value it might have had. What is a major obstacle in the relations between so many pairs of powers, territorial ambitions by one which adversely affect the other, is in this case virtually nonexistent.

There have always been a large number of controversies under discussion between the Department of State and the British Foreign Office. But the tendency to argue each dispute as a case to be settled by reference to principles of law testifies to the basically peaceful frame of reference within which the bickering was carried on. The long history of Anglo-American arbitrations from the time of the Jay Treaty of 1794 to our own day is evidence.

Although geography and technology drove Britain to seek more friendly relations with both Japan and the United States at the dawn of the twentieth century, the very different histories of the alliance between England and Japan, on the one hand, and of the spontaneous Anglo-American collaboration in two wars, on the other, suggest how much shared moral conceptions facilitate political collaboration. The Anglo-Japanese alliance was firm in peace but useless in war;* the improved Anglo-American relationship, which was not even based on a binding legal commitment, saved England from disaster in two wars.

The unregimented character of life in the two countries affects their relations in another way. There is a comparatively free penetration into the arena of public discussion of one country by the publicists of the other. Thus, appeals can be made over the heads of public officials to a public opinion which these officials cannot ignore. While this active intervention by individuals of one country in the discussions of public policy in the other enormously complicates and does not always improve Anglo-American relations, it offers additional protection to each country against an "anti-" policy by the other.

Similarity in democratic social organizations appears to have had a profound effect in preventing a ruinous Anglo-American naval rivalry after the First World War. Had Britain been as sensitive to the expansion of American naval power as she had earlier been to that of German naval power, Britain and America would have followed divergent paths after 1918. However, as Alfred Vagts has written, "civilian supremacy . . . reasserted itself strongly, brought about and carried through the Washington Conference and thereby led to 'a new order of sea power,' as the outcome of the era from 1918 to 1922 has been aptly called." [4]

Doubtless there were in 1921 men in the British and American navies who envisioned the other navy as the most probable next opponent. In each country these naval officers regarded the agreements made at the Washington Conference on the Limitation of Armaments in 1922 as a naval disaster for their own

* Japan was ostensibly an ally of Britain in the First World War, but her contribution to the defeat of Germany was small. She used the interval during which the other great powers were preoccupied in Europe: (1) to secure for herself the former German-held islands in the Western Pacific; (2) to make her famous Twenty-One Demands on China; and (3) to "help save Siberia from the Communists" by sending her own troops into that area.

country. That Anglo-American parity was no disaster for either is proved by the breast-beatings which were taking place on both sides of the Atlantic.[5]

Had the professional naval men in either country been permitted to determine policy, the Washington Conference might have had really catastrophic consequences. A continued naval race would have gravely jeopardized the possibility of Anglo-American joint action. The treaty of self-abnegation by which the United States and Great Britain bound themselves not to increase their fortifications in Western Pacific waters was a blunder based on an inadequate grasp of the expansionist basis of Japanese policy. It permitted Japan to emerge from the Conference with a free hand in the Western Pacific. Anglo-American competition, however, would have left her still freer, for each power would have been tempted to seek Japan's favor to offset the strength of the other.

It is now fashionable to assert that the Washington Conference was an Anglo-American disaster and a triumph for Japanese duplicity. Walter Lippmann in his recent *U. S. Foreign Policy* speaks of "the exorbitant folly of the Washington Disarmament Conference." He utters his *mea culpa* in unnecessarily emphatic tones when he says: "I followed the fashion . . . and denounced the admirals. . . . I am ashamed, all the more so because I had no excuse for not knowing better."[6] Had he been less fashionable and followed the admirals, he might today be equally unsatisfied with his earlier estimate of events. Neither the admirals nor the civilian negotiators had a clear conception of the complementary character of the British and American navies in the only foreseeable contingencies in which they would both be in action. Civilian leadership brought a halt to a disastrous naval competition. It was a triumph for the cause of Anglo-American co-operation.

This leadership, however, failed to capitalize on the great opportunity which presented itself to stabilize, without first going to war with Japan, the Western Pacific area. The tragedy was the failure to take jointly the steps which might have made the Pacific war unnecessary. The opportunity in this area, as in the European zone of conflict, to make a joint contribution to security arose from (1) the common nonexpansionist aims of the two foreign policies, and (2) the strategic interdependence of British and American territories.

The common quest for security (power not to be coerced) rather than for domination (power to coerce) insures that there is no fundamental conflict in policy. Cynics will, of course, say that the United States and Great Britain can afford to be non-aggressive because their territories have already been expanded to the point of satiety. It is true that Britain and America, as rich and peace-loving powers, have an especially great stake in a system of general security. To overstress the "territorially satisfied" aspect of their common policy, however, is to grant the validity of the outmoded "have vs. have-not" explanation of the causes of war. This is unnecessary and may be dangerous, for it implies that the Axis powers had grievances of such a character that they were entitled to plunge the world into war. The territorial satiety theory implies that such satiety is capable of objective determination, that a would-be great power which has not yet expanded to this objectively determined limit may be expected to do so, and that there is no more justice on the side of the defenders of the *status quo* than there is on the side of the aggressors. As a matter of fact, being a have-not power is almost exclusively the result of a nation's viewing itself as a have-not power. According to the "have vs. have-not" theory, Germany ought to have grown less aggressive with her successive expansions into the Saar, Austria, Czechoslovakia, and Memel. Her appetite, however, improved with eating.

Anglo-American opposition to aggression by other great states can be stated in moral terms, for they are willing to deny opportunities for imperial expansion to themselves as well as to others. They have discovered that to maintain or to restore or even to create local sovereignties—in Holland, Belgium,

Norway, the Philippine Islands, Iraq, etc.—is cheaper and, more important, in harmony with the public conscience of each nation. Provided the small state can keep the aggressor out, Great Britain and the United States have no reason even in areas strategically important to them to jeopardize its independence. A program to preserve the less powerful states accords with the civilized world's interest in reducing profitable aggression to the minimum.

Against the background of their common ethic, analyses of strategic interdependence take on new meaning. A demonstration that the two powers need each other would be a poor argument for joint policy except on the assumption that they can trust each other. Let us examine first the services which a friendly United States could render the British Commonwealth. In the Boer War, in 1914, and in 1939, Canada, Australia, and New Zealand followed the mother country into war. Until the fall of Singapore had revealed the poverty of British power in the Far East, Australia and New Zealand were prepared to pay the price of unquestioning support for Britain in her conflict in Europe, in return counting upon British sea power to keep the teeming hordes of Asia from their shores.[7] War has demonstrated that United States help is indispensable in the protection of these isolated Dominions. Only a Britain which can with certainty count upon American support in case of renewed general war can continue to evoke the spontaneous collaboration of Australia * and New Zealand.

Canadian support of British policy in three wars within a half century has been ungrudging, but it has become less a matter of course. As that Dominion's sense of nationhood has grown, it has wished to make an independent evaluation of policy. The Canadian government has in advance of war steadfastly refused to be consulted regarding decisions in British

---

* Australian Gallup Polls report that 82 per cent of the Australians interviewed favored a permanent alliance between the United States and the British Empire. "Australia Speaks," Nos. 153-61, October, 1943.

foreign policy in order not to be committed to support Great Britain when the crisis occurred. She entered the war against Nazi Germany, but by delaying the formal declaration of war for a week, until September 10, 1939, she informed Britain and the world that the decision registered her own free choice. Canada's case differs sharply from that of Australia and New Zealand in that the territorial integrity of her homeland is underwritten by the United States,* and British sea power will not protect her from the United States. The reason is different, but the effect is the same: Canada's Commonwealth tie could not long survive a failure of Anglo-American collaboration. One of the most powerful guarantors against a contracting Commonwealth is American partnership in its preservation.

The world in general and Britain's present and prospective allies in particular have been impressed by the fact that the Dominions, and especially Canada, did stand behind the mother country in her hour of peril. In the lonely period after June, 1940, Canada was in fact the second most powerful of the nations fighting the Axis. When, therefore, Great Britain makes and receives commitments in the field of high politics, her value as an ally is enhanced by a general belief in her capacity to evoke co-operation from the transoceanic British nations. Without the support of the Dominions, Britain's declining political role would be even more sharply emphasized. She could hardly claim to be more than a regional European power of the same order of importance as the larger states across the Channel.

For the British there can be no equally satisfactory substitute for support by the United States. It is conceivable that in a few years air power will bring the American continental base within reach of a European enemy. However, there is no conceivable enemy of Britain and America which could encompass

---

* By the Kingston speech of President Roosevelt, August 18, 1938, and the Ogdensburg Agreement of August 18, 1940, what had long been implicit was made explicit. Canada and the United States are joined in what may now be described as a "North American security union."

the final defeat of the United States until after Britain's island-fortress had first collapsed. For Britain, this means that the American arsenal of matériel and the American reservoir of personnel will be elements of strength as long as there is a Britain to benefit from their existence.

In summary, Britain's status as a first-rank power is contingent upon support from the self-governing Dominions and from the United States. The support of the former can be counted on only if the support of the latter seems assured; therefore, Britain's position is doubly dependent on American good will.* Unless the United States has equally powerful reasons for seeking British collaboration, the day of the Anglo-Saxon as a prime mover in world politics would seem to be at a close. What is the evidence that the efficient conduct of American foreign policy demands Anglo-American co-operation?

For the United States, on the assumption of Anglo-American collaboration, the necessity for an enemy to reduce the British base in the course of a victorious war against the United States gives this country a huge military stake in the preservation of British independence. We have an additional stake in Great Britain's island-base because it offers a unique opportunity for American power to make its influence felt on the other side of the ocean. If it is a valid objective of American policy to keep war out of our own continental homeland, then an ally whose territories furnish bases from which any new European aggressor could be kept within Europe is indeed a valuable ally. Her home island is an offshore bastion inherently strong enough to

* Field Marshal Smuts' "explosive" speech of November 25, 1943, and Lord Halifax's Toronto speech of January 24, 1944, were apparently engendered by a sense of Britain's declining power position and a belief in the necessity of checking that decline. In a sense the two proposals provide alternatives to Britain's growing dependence on American power. Smuts called for closer collaboration between Britain and the powers on the western fringe of Europe. These are also the African colonial powers, and it is thus apparent that Smuts was advocating a policy for both Britain and South Africa. Halifax urged a closer political integration of Great Britain and the Dominions.

defend itself until American aid has time to arrive in force and large enough to provide a base for a full-scale offensive. For the United States, too, there can be no substitute.

In a sense, Great Britain is the "sole buyer" of American military might. America's war potential is too small for her to stand alone against the world, but it is too great to be applied, in an hour of crisis, only in this hemisphere.[8] Unless it is transmitted through Britain to the world's main zone of conflict, the United States can do little to control its own destiny.

This conclusion is reinforced by an examination of other points at which British and American military assets complement each other. Throughout the world the United States is finding it necessary to "borrow" parts of the British Empire in order to conduct war against the Axis. India, Australia, and New Zealand are rear bases for the offensive against Japan, and most of the Pacific islands which are forward bases are parts of the Empire. The roads to victory in Tunisia and Sicily led through Gibraltar and around the Cape of Good Hope. British control of strong points in the Middle East kept the way open for American supplies to reach the Soviet Union through Iran. If the present war is to be for Americans a war of no annexations, as the Atlantic Charter promises, then these key areas will remain outside American sovereignty and will have to be "borrowable" if the United States is after this war to act effectively to prevent future general wars.*

In summary, both Britain and Britain's Empire are essential to American security because they provide the indispensable bases from which threats to the United States from Old World aggressors can be stopped within the Old World. American war potential plus British "locational" assets make a formidable

---

* This does not necessarily mean that the United States must underwrite the integrity of the whole British Empire. It does mean that there will be areas in addition to the United Kingdom and Canada in which there is an American interest in upholding the British position.

combination throughout the seven seas and about the fringes of the Eurasian land mass.

A security policy developed on the assumption of a fundamental community of interest permits American and British military assets to complement each other in another way. It permits a regional specialization by each power. The main body of United States capital-ship strength has been in the Pacific Ocean for nearly a generation. This disposition of ships has reflected the conviction of our government that with British naval power dominant in European waters a major concentration of American naval units in the North Atlantic would be superfluous. It was not the building of the Panama Canal that made a "two-ocean" navy unnecessary for the United States but fundamental agreement with a Britain whose navy dominated the Atlantic shores of Europe. Once Japan had embarked on her program of imperial expansion, it was clear that British interests in the Western Pacific were supported less by British than by American power. War in the Pacific has proved to be an American war. East of the line which divides the commands of General MacArthur and Lord Mountbatten, Empire security will almost certainly continue to depend on United States strength.*

British interests in the Western Atlantic, the Caribbean, and the New World generally have not been supported by units of the British navy for forty years. The basic pattern thus emerges of an informal global collaboration in which the Western Atlantic, the New World, and the Pacific Ocean area are primary United States responsibilities, with Western Europe, the Mediterranean, the Middle East, and the Indian Ocean left in the first instance to British protection.

* If the liquidation of Japanese military power is complete, the Antipodean Dominions may find themselves for a period in a "no-great-power" zone, and their present sense of dependence on the United States may decline sharply. With renewed crisis, the United States would again be asked to underwrite their security.

In a world in which no nation, however strong, can protect itself against every imaginable contingency by its own efforts alone, this efficient division of labor permits a maximum utilization of United States and British Empire resources. Since the peoples involved seek security with the least possible reduction of their standard of living, both partners should wish to see the economies of jointly planned policy preserved.

For the United States this discussion of strategic interdependence leads to one conclusion which, at the risk of repetition, will be restated: Maximum security for the United States requires Britain's continued existence as a strong power. "Aid to Britain" is in reality "aid to the United States." Efforts of the United States to assume a role of constructive world leadership have frequently been frustrated by confusion over that fact.

For both powers, maximum security requires that expansionist aggression be made expensive and unprofitable. The leaders of the two powers, however, have not always agreed how their common task should be divided between them. Although both have wished to see the cat belled, each has in recent crises been anxious for the other to take more of the risk.*

In the Americas the United States has been more than willing to assume the whole burden, and for a half century Great Britain has not opposed this. In Asia the United States rather lightly undertook a share in the opening-up of China and Japan. Since the acquisition of the Philippine Islands, it has not had the option of withdrawing. In Europe, however, its participation has been intermittent and generally reluctant. The United States has been as reluctant to commit itself in advance to participate in "Europe's quarrels"—a phrase which itself implies "a plague on both your houses" and which puts aggressor and victim of aggression on a plane of moral equality—as Great Britain has in recent years been anxious to have its own security underwritten.

* Where there has been confusion as to which cat required belling, the problem has been further complicated. See *infra*, Chapters V and VI.

STRATEGIC INTERDEPENDENCE

It is, therefore, not surprising that, in the onward march of the aggressors during the 'thirties, groups in each country placed responsibility for successive Axis diplomatic triumphs on the government of the other.* The United States would take no step which involved the risk of immediate war. To the aggressors it seemed to indicate that it was safe to count on a period of American nonparticipation in war in the event that Britain and France challenged them. To these latter countries it served as a warning that they might for a time have to face the Axis with no help from the United States.†

For the "sell-out" of Ethiopia, Loyalist Spain, and Czechoslovakia, American liberals bitterly denounced the British government. British conservatives could only retort that Americans had no right to criticize the Munich Pact unless they had been prepared to have their country come to Britain's aid in the event that Hitler made war. There is no longer valid reason to pass judgment on the comparative blameworthiness of the two policies. The failure of British and American policies to be coordinated for the implementation of common objectives was, however, a contributing factor to the return of general war after only twenty years of peace.

The decreasing material benefits of Empire, decreasing largely because the democratic ethic of both Britain and the United States now forbids ruthless exploitation, and the declining relative strength of Britain in Europe make it certain that the British will press for the United States to assume additional burdens in guaranteeing world order. Two world wars have demonstrated that American help will be forthcoming. But in both wars the British have felt that they had to go on

---

* Cf. *supra*, pp. 37-38, and *infra*, pp. 134-38 and p. 168, n. 10. Secretary of State Stimson's book, *The Far Eastern Crisis*, New York, Harpers, 1936, stimulated controversy in both countries as to where the real responsibility for the fiasco of collective security lay in the Manchurian crisis.

† It would be unfair to those formulating American policy to suggest that the body of American public opinion was anxious to have the United States assume a more vigorous role than it actually played.

too long alone and had to come too close to defeat for this pattern to be repeated a third time. Next time they will want guarantees not against defeat but against having to stem the flood of aggression alone for a long period. Britain will want assurance that the United States will send, under certain circumstances, immediate aid in the event of renewed aggression in Europe west of the Soviet Union. This demand will conflict with the long American tradition of "no prior commitments." Failure to resolve the conflict between Britain's needs and America's tradition may doom Europe to chaos and ourselves to the continued threat of war.

One way to avoid the conflict would be to let each succeeding crisis demonstrate the common interests of the two powers. However, an unrecognized community of interest is not a basis for efficient collaboration. It may be sufficient to guarantee Britain against final defeat in a general war, although even this is not certain. Another time the United States might wait too long. It is not enough to prevent the emergence of a new crisis situation. Only security policies co-ordinated in advance of the crisis of general war have any chance of preventing that crisis from taking place.

Common traditions and the greater similarity of security objectives will make Anglo-American collaboration more intimate than the collaboration between these two and the Soviet Union.[9] Before one discusses any special Anglo-American security arrangements, the essential character of Soviet co-operation needs again to be emphasized. A type of Anglo-American collaboration which provoked unnecessary Soviet hostility would have to be rejected. The Soviet Union is too big to be excluded from the innermost circles of peace planning.

The first line of defense for American and British security is the maintenance of the territorial integrity of Germany's immediate neighbors; and this first line can be easily breached if Soviet and Anglo-American policies sharply diverge. Even Soviet indifference would jeopardize British and American peace plans. Sea power, in an age of substitutes and synthetics, no longer finds it easy to strangle the industrial economies of Western Europe by shutting off supplies from overseas. It would completely lose its effectiveness if the industries and industrial populations of Europe could draw on the vast resources of a neutral Soviet Eurasia. Air power, too, would find its task enormously complicated if German military effort could concentrate on anti-aircraft defense to the exclusion of military operations in the East. If the Soviet Union should exclude itself from joint planning to preserve the peace, the case would be different. Only after that event has taken place would maximum security lie along a road which the Soviet Union was not traveling also.

There would be no security at all in a type of collaboration which brought into being an anti-Anglo-American coalition that would not otherwise have been formed. The reactions of the Soviet Union and of the small countries would vary according to the slogans used to justify Anglo-American co-operation. If the necessity for it is stated in arrogant terms which imply the superiority of the Anglo-Saxon, the reaction will certainly be unfavorable. Secretary of State Olney's reference to "patriotism of race," Joseph Chamberlain's plea for an Anglo-American-German "three-cousin system," Senator Beveridge's dictum that God had "made the English-speaking and Teutonic peoples the master organizers of the world," [10] all show the real affinity in basic conception between Pan-Germanism and "race"-inspired schemes for Anglo-American hegemony. Lionel Gelber indicates the real disservice which racists have done to Anglo-American unity when he writes:

Yet, for that [scorn of Anglo-American co-operation as a new form of the myth of racial superiority], blame must be borne by public men who orate unreflectingly about healing the schism between the sundered branches of the Anglo-Saxon race. . . . The English-speaking peoples were least friendly when the population of the United States—from the American Revolution to the Spanish War of 1898—most nearly approximated in "Anglo-Saxon" ethnological make-up. ... For the identity of interest ... derives from a common heritage of liberty into which all may enter. . . .[11]

Scarcely less objectionable to the non-Anglo-Saxon world is the attitude illustrated by Lady Astor's invitation to the Russians and Chinese, calling upon them to co-operate with Britons and Americans "if they adopt our way of thinking."

Without doubt, some have proposed an Anglo-American alliance in order to reject the form but preserve the substance of the now unpopular isolationism. William Randolph Hearst advocated such an alliance as an alternative to Woodrow Wilson's League of Nations, and J. L. Garvin called for an American orientation in British policy in order to avoid for Britain the necessity of making commitments in Europe.[12]

Collaboration in the name of preserving Western democracy from communism is equally dangerous. Such a collaboration would revive the Soviet nightmare of encirclement and would provoke a violent reaction, perhaps in the form of more active intervention in the affairs of its immediate neighbors with a view to their more complete incorporation into the Soviet security system.

If, however, the habit of Anglo-American collaboration develops and is justified by reference to their joint interest in something impersonal like "freedom," including the freedom of nations not to be enslaved by aggressors, the dangers of countercollaboration against Britain and America would be reduced.* For the people of the United States this means enlarging the symbol "U.S.A." so that it includes, for certain purposes, Great Britain and the Dominions. "We" must in certain types of international political crisis include the British as

* The Teheran Declaration dedicates the two Western powers, and their Soviet ally also, to the "elimination of tyranny and slavery, oppression and intolerance" and envisions a "day when all the peoples of the world may live free lives untouched by tyranny and according to their varying desires and their own consciences."

a matter of course. "Aid to Britain" must become "aid to us." Lend-lease and reverse lend-lease with their implied invitations to calculate comparative advantage and sacrifice demonstrate how *not* to justify collaboration. But it must be Britons as co-lovers of freedom and security, not as co-warriors against communism, that are included within the broadened conception of "us."

There is another factor which sets a limit to the degree of intimacy in the Anglo-American relationship. It is spelled out by John Strachey in his *Federalism or Socialism?* [13] He opposes all schemes for "federal union" or other organic constitutional connection between the United States and the British Commonwealth on the ground that it would limit the progress of social planning in Britain to the slower pace of socialization in the United States.

Even in the absence of a special constitutional tie, divergent domestic political programs limit the extent of collaboration in foreign affairs. Thus, an important instrument for waging a coalition war, the Franco-British Financial Agreement of December, 1939, which called for a fixing of the sterling-franc exchange rate, required each country to use its own funds to support the other's currency in the officially controlled exchanges. This, however, would ultimately have required parallel policies to combat inflation, e.g., in the matters of taxes, wage limitations, and control of excess profits. The failure of swings in the political pendulums of England and the United States to synchronize during the postwar period may make impracticable some of the more ambitious proposals for joint leadership in the new era.

Irrespective of the motivation or objectives of a joint program, the determination to collaborate will have to be registered in some form; for co-operation in advance of crisis, it has already been argued, requires some form of commitment. The form may be a great deal less important than the fact of collaboration. Nevertheless, unless a form for collaborating is found which does not inhibit the process of collaboration, the latter is bound to fail. Assurance of aid in the event of renewed European aggression might or might not take the form of an exclusively Anglo-American agreement.

A bilateral defense pact, however, is open to a number of objections, including the following:

(1) Spontaneous and separate estimates of the national interests of the two countries will make for parallel policy in any case.

(2) An exclusive arrangement might seem to the world to rest upon a "blood is thicker than water" basis and would thus have unfortunate connotations at a time when we are engaged in a struggle against racism in all its forms.

(3) An exclusive arrangement might provoke an anti-Anglo-American coalition or, at the very least, inhibit full co-operation from the other nations with which the United States and Great Britain are united by their common devotion to free institutions.

(4) The Soviet Union should not be excluded from the innermost circle of the peace planners, at least as long as it is willing to be included in that circle. Furthermore, the Soviet Union's military assets so complement those of Britain and the United States that its importance as a partner is even greater than that indicated by reference to its size and strength.

(5) Large sections of American opinion are traditionally hostile to bilateral "entangling" alliances. This is especially true of an Anglo-American arrangement, for Anglophobia is most rife among politically important minorities.

(6) Because of its geographic position, Great Britain has no choice but to be a defender of America from a continental European aggressor. An alliance would not increase the probability that it would act in the way Americans want it to, since it will do so in any case.

(7) To many Americans an Anglo-American alliance would be interpreted as more "aid to Britain." Actually, the chief

justification for a special commitment to Britain is that it is "aid to ourselves" since a reduction of our British advanced base would deal an irreparable blow to our defense system.

(8) The common devotion of Great Britain and the United States to the maintenance of "freedom," including the freedom of peoples everywhere in the world not to be enslaved by aggressors, can best be registered in an instrument which is open to the signatures of the representatives of all free peoples. Such an appropriate instrument would be a multilateral agreement setting up the general security organization envisioned in the Moscow Declaration.

It is nevertheless important that some formal statement of the American interest in a friendly and independent Britain be made in terms so explicit that it will be understood throughout the world. The advantages of placing such a statement in the public record of our time are many.

(1) Would-be aggressors have twice in a quarter century underestimated the American interest in a free Britain. We therefore have had to establish our interest by fighting when we might possibly have established it by demonstrating in advance our willingness to fight. What is needed is to discourage the aggressor's challenging the postwar order in hope of quick victory before the United States should again bring effective aid.

(2) Staff conversations to co-ordinate American and British military and naval policy toward the achievement of common objectives cannot well be based upon an informal estimate by the professional military men of the degree of informal collaboration which is thought to exist between the two Foreign Offices. They ought not and cannot be expected to act except on the basis of some more precise formulation of common interest. Only on such a basis could maximum assistance be rendered to an England which the United States wished to defend. On this firm political foundation American military authorities could build a military machine which stressed the fully transferable

components of power and thus could be brought speedily to the support of the transatlantic advance base.

(3) A unilateral declaration of American interest in a friendly and independent Britain would base any commitment to Britain on the firm basis of the United States' own interest.

(4) A unilateral declaration of a special United States interest in a particular area is in the best American tradition. By the Monroe Doctrine our interest in a friendly and independent Latin America was formally brought to the attention of the world. More recently, President Roosevelt in his Kingston speech of August 18, 1938, stated in unmistakable terms our interest in a friendly and independent Canada when he said:

The Dominion of Canada is part of the sisterhood of the British Empire. I give to you assurance that the people of the United States will not stand idly by if domination of Canadian soil is threatened by any other Empire.[14]

Paraphrasing President Monroe, the President of the United States might on the occasion of his annual message to Congress or at some other moment of high ceremonial significance make an analogous declaration regarding the United Kingdom. He might for example declare:

We owe it, therefore, to candor and to the amicable relations which we hope will long persist between ourselves and the powers of Europe to declare that we should consider any attempt on their part to extend their dominion to any portion of the British Isles as dangerous to our peace and safety. We could not view any interposition for the purpose of oppressing them, or controlling in any manner their destiny, by any European power in any other light than as the manifestation of an unfriendly disposition toward the United States.

To be fully effective the President's words should contain some reference to Britain's invincibility. Without such a reference, the declaration might create the painful impression in England that the United States was relegating that country to the status of a second-rank power which was in especial need of guarantees. If the British government were given an opportunity to make an analogous declaration regarding its intention to support United States' interests in the Western Pacific, this impression might be avoided. If the declaration were followed by some joint pronouncement from the Anglo-American Combined Chiefs of Staff indicating that their activities would continue beyond the war period, the mutuality of the Anglo-American relationship would be further demonstrated.

To give further solemnity to this declaration, it might be reinforced by the adoption of a Senate resolution which incorporated the key phrases of the President's pronouncement into the text of its own resolution. There should of course be no attempt to secure the passage of such a resolution unless it could be accomplished without prolonged and acrimonious debate and unless there should be advance assurance of its adoption by an overwhelming and nonpartisan majority.

The English-speaking peoples have, so far as their foreign policies are concerned, many more compelling reasons for collaboration than "the common heritage" to which orators in both countries so often refer. A specific proposal has been made for enlarging the symbol, "United States," so that it refers, for security purposes at least, to the United States plus Great Britain. Can it be further enlarged to include the Soviet Union?

PART THREE

THE WESTERN POWERS AND
THE SOVIET UNION

V. Forecasting Soviet Policy

The last and highest triumph of history would, to his mind, be the bringing of Russia into the Atlantic combine, and the just and fair allotment of the whole world among the regulated activities of the universe.   "Education of Henry Adams"

IN a single detail Henry Adams was profoundly wrong. He believed it easier to win German than Russian collaboration.[1] History has twice in a generation proved Adams' error. In making this error he was in a numerous and well-placed company. Artificers of British foreign policy both in Adams' generation and in our own have wooed German favor in order that they should not have to face their *bête noire*, the Russian bear, alone.[2] His sense of the sequence of coming events failed him; but he discovered, sooner than his contemporaries, that one key to general peace lay in the relationship of the Western democracies to Russia.

The strategic interdependence of Great Britain and the United States is so great that for many purposes it is permissible to speak of these Western democracies as if they constituted a single power-nucleus. The United States may possibly again experience a mood of withdrawal, in which event London would temporarily appear to be the policy-center of the West. In a fresh crisis, however, the stake of the United States in Britain's survival would again be made manifest. Washington would again assume a central position of leadership. Alternatively, if the American government self-consciously and continuously participates in the politics of the postwar world, Great Britain may appear as the least of the Big Three and therefore the one upon which the two biggest, in their quest for dependable allies, concentrate the heaviest pressure. In either case, although British power and American power may be imperfectly co-ordinated, the expectation is that in a new conflict the armed might of these two countries would be thrown into the scales on the same side.

In bringing Anglo-American power to bear in a world in which the Soviet Union also has great military power, British and American leaders cannot escape basing foreign policy upon some estimate regarding the future use to which Soviet power will be put. They have carefully to calculate the risk of acting as if they expected Soviet policy to be highly expansionist, geographically or ideologically or both, as against the risk of acting as if they expected it to be nonexpansionist or only moderately expansionist.[3] Statesmen in our time will have no more responsible task than weighing these risks.

Note that they are called upon to act "as if." Statesmen cannot simply fashion policy to meet the most probable event in a world in which the improbable frequently occurs. They must act on one basis but have alternate courses of action laid out in case earlier calculations prove erroneous. Since the future is subject to influences beyond one's own control, policy must be based on multiple contingencies. In the event that the Western powers have no policy at all in case the "most probable" contingency fails to occur, the "most probable" would probably not occur. They must not put all their eggs in one basket.

They must, however, put a good many of them, tentatively at least, in one basket. They cannot avoid acting on the basis of some assumption about Soviet policy, however imperfect may be the information now available for verifying that assumption.

Even without the gift of perfect prevision, action which cannot be postponed may as well be based on a more rather than a less sophisticated assumption.

We know that Soviet foreign policy is not being evolved in a vacuum. A careful reading of Russian history and a detailed analysis of published debates in which the Communist "party line" in matters of foreign affairs is discussed will no doubt yield significant clues.[4] It would, however, do scant honor to the intellectual processes of Soviet statesmen to suppose that the course of Soviet policy follows an inflexible and undeviating line. It is obviously based on some calculation about the policy to be pursued by the strongest power outside Russia, the United States. There are some features of American policy which it is in the American interest and in the Soviet Union's to make plain at the outset. Is the United States itself expansionist? *

There can be little doubt that Americans are by and large opposed to a program of territorial aggrandizement for the United States. Their position on the question of Philippine independence suggests that the slogans of imperialism have lost their power to quicken the patriotic impulses of the country. Future expansion must be of a reluctant and preventive character. It must be justified in terms like "responsibility."

America therefore need not adopt a foreign policy whose implementation would require regimentation at home and allies abroad sufficient to allow territorial expansion at will. If the United States does not regard the world as its oyster, it does, however, wish to make certain that it will not be the oyster of any other part of the world. It must seek to reduce the

---

* Although it is correct for certain purposes to treat the Anglo-American combination as a single aggregation of power, it is the United States more than Great Britain which is hesitant about its long-run policy toward the Soviet Union. It may, therefore, be an American decision which will determine the way in which the Soviet and Anglo-American concentrations of power accommodate themselves to each other's existence.

"threat value" of its neighbors, near and far, great and small.*
If this course of action would be furthered by reducing its own
threat value to some of them, a nonexpansionist United States
might be expected to renounce the opportunity for successful
aggression on its own part.

The most important of these neighbors is not the nearest,
but it is the greatest, the Soviet Union. The great distance between the major seats of Soviet power and those of the United
States permits each to adopt toward the other a policy based
on the tentative assumption that the other does not seek to encompass its downfall and establish a world-wide hegemony.
For any quest for world hegemony or unlimited territorial
aggrandizement would reveal itself long before it was an immediate threat to the other. Americans would be sensitive to
the implications of any increase in Soviet territories and would
speedily react to any aggrandizement so great that it threatened
the encirclement of the American homeland. Furthermore,
since the efficacy of military power is much reduced by having
to be applied from a distance, the temptation for even a super-

---

* "Threat value" is a term borrowed from the naturalistic vocabulary of H. D. Lasswell. In his analysis, the "self" concerning which calculations of power relationships are made in international politics is normally the nation-state. Under certain circumstances, this "self" may become narrower than the nation-state as in civil war, or broader than the nation-state as in the case of the United States-Canadian "security union," or it may transcend national boundaries as in the case of world revolution. In the international politics of our time, a few great powers are the significant "selves." To say that the United States seeks "to reduce the threat value" of its great neighbors is to say that this particular self seeks to minimize the chance that it might be annihilated or successfully coerced by another power or combination of powers. This is not identical with the goal of certain other significant selves, e.g., Nazi Germany, which in its calculation of power relationships seeks to maximize the chance that it may annihilate or successfully coerce other powers. The United States may be said to seek "security"; Nazi Germany, "domination."

For a fundamental analysis of the structure of world politics in our time see Professor Lasswell's *World Politics and Personal Insecurity*, New York, McGraw-Hill, 1935.

power to aggress upon a powerful and distant state must be slight.

The problem of American foreign policy is not to create a situation in which the United States could successfully commit an act of aggression against the Soviet Union but rather to minimize the possible disregard of its own national interests. It is in the American interest to see a Soviet Union whose great energies are devoted to improving the welfare of its own people and not to enlarging the domain of the Soviet Union nor to provoking world revolution. We have already rejected the thesis that Soviet policy represents the inexorable unfolding of patterns of action long since determined upon. Other things being equal, the least risky policy for the United States is that which encourages the nonexpansionist forces within the Soviet Union.

There are policies which, if adopted as the official policies of this country, would provoke Soviet intransigence and, in all probability, a "defensive" expansionism. The lesson of the last quarter century in this regard is clear. The Soviet leadership declared, and it was widely believed, that the capitalist powers, especially France and Britain, were seeking to combine against the Soviet Union. That country was continually "blackballed" in the exclusive club of the inner decision-making powers. In conferences at Versailles, Washington, Locarno, Stresa, and Munich, the Soviet Union was the uninvited "pariah" power. The last of these conferences completely destroyed Soviet diplomatic defenses in Europe. All this could have been justified only on the assumption that Soviet Russia was the chief potential aggressor, whatever hypocritical "peace is indivisible" tactic her leaders might at the moment be pursuing. It is not surprising that at the outset of the present war the Soviet government chose to turn the conflict to the West by making a pact with Hitlerite Germany.

There is also without doubt a course of action for the United States so supine as to invite Soviet disregard of American vital interests. Either course of action would enhance the probability of war as the arbiter of Soviet-American disputes and lessen the probability of American success in the event of conflict. Between these two extremes, there may be a set of policies which give maximum protection to the American national interest, including the interest in avoiding an unnecessary conflict.

We are now ready to restate the rather simple question: "Ought American and British policy to be based on the assumption of an expansionist or a nonexpansionist Soviet Union?" The question has now become: "What course of action by the Western powers minimizes the likelihood of a Soviet policy which the United States and Britain would find it necessary to oppose by war?"

In the nineteenth century British and American diplomatic relations with Russia were in no way similar. British statesmen assumed that it was Russian power which had to be checked if Europe were to be kept in balance. The vocabulary of Sir Halford Mackinder, who grew up during the period of British preoccupation with Russian expansion, with its emphasis on the struggle between land power and sea power, reflected and served to dramatize the Anglo-Russian struggle.[5] Land power, emanating from the Russian heartland, thrust itself southwestward into the Balkans and reached especially for the control of the Bosphorus and the Dardanelles. Southward also it expanded to fill the void left by the contracting power of the Ottoman Empire. To the southeast it pushed, seeking to extend Russian influence in Persia and, through Afghanistan, upon the northwest frontiers of India. Against expansion in any of these directions British diplomacy was active, for at every point Russian advance seemed to threaten the "life line of Empire."

Transfixed by the prospect of a more powerful Russia, English statesmen only reluctantly and belatedly adopted measures after 1900 to check the rising power of Germany. British measures to improve relations with the United States and Japan by recognizing the paramount interest of each in its own region have been described. With the formation of a Franco-British diplomatic entente in 1904, the way was opened naturally for a reconsideration of relations with France's Russian ally. The ineffective performance of Russian armed forces in the Russo-Japanese war cast some doubt on whether Czarist Russia was the menace it had generally been considered to be. The Czar's promises of constitutional reform in the wake of the Russian defeat and the opening of the first Russian Duma disposed British opinion more favorably. The Balkans and Turkey were not for the moment acute sources of friction, and the areas of conflict were now to the east in Persia, Afghanistan, and Tibet. An Anglo-Russian treaty of 1907 liquidated those difficulties. Most of the barriers to an Anglo-Russian partnership in the First World War against Germany and the Central Powers had now disappeared, although the cloud of Pan-Slavism still hung over amicable relations. The idea of an inherent incompatibility between British and Russian policies was becoming obsolete. In the face of an attempt to unify Europe by a third power, Germany, their interests merged and have in our own time merged again.

In contrast to the stormy course of Anglo-Russian diplomacy, relations between the United States and Russia were in the nineteenth century seldom disturbed.[6] Russian leadership in the Holy Alliance, which was suspected of planning to restore the revolting colonies of Spain to Spanish rule, and Russia's southward advances along the west coast of North America brought Russia into conflict with two of the three principles enunciated in the Monroe Doctrine, nonintervention in American affairs and nonextension of colonial possessions. British opposition to intervention in the revolt of the Spanish colonies prevented the first from becoming a source of actual Russian-American conflict. By treaties of 1824 and 1825 with the United States and Britain respectively, Russia signified her intention not to establish new colonies in the Northwest and agreed to a southern limit for Alaska. This prevented possible conflict with the United States over the second principle laid down by Monroe. With United States purchase of Alaska in 1867 the chance of Russian-American conflict over New World affairs was further reduced. Although the outer limits of their respective territories now approach each other in the Bering Strait, they do so only in sparsely inhabited and economically unimportant areas. In the years before the First World War, the two powers developed policies with respect to North China and Manchuria which were not wholly compatible, but there was at no time a serious threat of war.

Geography has favored Russian-American friendship. The threat value of each to the other would now be much greater if the main centers of population and industrial power were not so widely separated. By the same token geography has made possible the most complete expression of distaste for each other's system, since red-baiting in the one country and "white"-baiting in the other were valuable techniques for consolidating power internally at small risk externally.

Disputes between the two countries not related to their contrasting ideologies have for the most part long been forgotten. Specific disputes growing out of the Russian Revolution, e.g., claims by the United States for its expropriated nationals and for bondholders who had loaned money to the Imperial Russian Government and counterclaims by the Soviet Union for damages resulting from the prolongation of civil war due to Allied intervention after the First World War, have tended to become obsolete. Dormant but capable of speedy resuscitation are conflicts based on the charge of ideological intervention by Soviet-controlled communist parties in the internal politics of the United States and its neighbors in Latin America, as well as in the political struggles of China and the colonial world. Reflecting a fundamental distrust were the intensity of the indignation which the Soviet Union's unfortunate Winter War with Finland aroused and the extreme recklessness of proposals to aid Finland.* Many proposals advocated policies which would have driven the U.S.S.R. into war on the side of the Axis.

Even in the midst of war the most violent Russophobia occasionally manifests itself. Max Eastman, for example, in the leading article in a widely read magazine, wrote: "Those eager to be fooled about Russia make eloquent pleas for Stalin's 'good faith.' But Bolsheviks do not believe *even theoretically* in good faith." [7] Senator Chandler stated in a much publicized speech to the United States Senate that "we have a friend . . . who is lending aid and comfort to the enemy" and that the failure of the U.S.S.R. to grant the United States bases in Siberia from which to bomb Japan has "cost us . . . lives . . . [and] will put gold stars on many a mother's flag." [8] When even in war time a minority opinion of this character regarding one's ally finds prominent public expression, that ally may allow for the possibility that in the postwar period the minority may become a majority. This does not mean that Americans should develop a wholly uncritical attitude toward Soviet policy. If, however, they desire to avoid unnecessary war with the Soviet Union, their public expressions ought to demonstrate a friendly attitude toward a Soviet Union which seeks security rather than domination.

The monolithic structure of Soviet society offers small scope for ideological intervention within its borders. Slogans are exported, not imported. The Soviet fear is therefore not of ideological but of military and financial pressure. During the interwar period, before it had become clear that some of the "capitalist plutocracies" would be its partners in a great "patriotic war" against Hitlerite Germany, the Western powers, democratic and fascist alike, were accused of conspiring to en-

* See e.g., Hanson W. Baldwin, *United We Stand!*, New York, McGraw-Hill, 1941, pp. 10-12. Even this trained military analyst characterized the failure of the Allies to aid Finland in 1940 as "an unforeseeable and magnificent opportunity . . . completely muffed."

circle the Soviet Union. Soviet leaders were especially sensitive to real or fancied intervention from the West in the affairs of the U.S.S.R.'s nearest neighbors.* They were naturally anxious that the border states which separated the U.S.S.R. from the other great powers in Europe not be used as advance bases in a great anti-Soviet coalition. In the postwar as in the prewar period the Soviet Union will watch with close attention the impact of any Anglo-American policy along its borders.

Perhaps to counter pressure from the West it will insist on "friendly regimes" in the former East European *cordon sanitaire* or even on full sovietization of part of that area. The U.S.S.R. has bound itself to permit the creation of a "strong and independent Poland," [9] but the rupture of diplomatic relations with the Polish government-in-exile, the appointment of Alexander Korneichuk, the husband of Wanda Wasilewska, the head of the Moscow-sponsored "Union of Polish Patriots," to the position of Commissar for Foreign Affairs of the Ukrainian Socialist Soviet Republic, and the formation of the Polish National Council in Soviet territory, cast doubt on the proper interpretation of this self-denying pledge.

The substantial body of persons of Polish and Lithuanian descent in key political areas in the United States strenuously opposes formal acquiescence by any American government in increased Soviet hegemony in East and Central Europe. The hard nucleus of Roman Catholic anti-communist opinion in this country also makes difficult any concession to Soviet demands. On the other hand, the basic power situation presented to Britain and America by a Soviet Union whose Red Army is just completing the annihilation of Hitler's legions hardly justifies such an attitude. In a realistic view, the Soviet Union may or may not demonstrate moderation in the use of its great

* Even during the present war the Soviet government has demonstrated its anxiety on this score. Cf. New York *Times*, October 15, 1943, for a report that Stalin is uneasy lest the expanding United States forces in Iran remain after peace has been re-established.

military and ideological power to coerce its near neighbors, but its decision in this matter is not one which we can *directly* oppose. Whether there is anything which Britain and America can do to influence Soviet policy in the direction of moderation will be discussed later. Only after alleviating Soviet fears of ultimate military encirclement will the Western powers get a sympathetic hearing for any proposals which they may wish to put forward regarding Eastern Europe.

Meanwhile, the Soviet Union is prepared to act to defend with vigor what it conceives to be its own best interests and is even prepared to pursue a policy which will alienate British and American good will if those interests could be best forwarded by such action. This is so obvious that it will not disturb that increasing element of American opinion which follows with intelligent interest the development of Soviet relations with its allies. Americans have long been accustomed to the idea that American foreign policy is designed to further America's best interests. They usually believe that these interests do not conflict with the legitimate interests of the rest of the world. They are gradually accustoming themselves to the idea that other great states also act in line with their own interests and that these interests do not necessarily conflict with the legitimate interests of the United States.

Except for Communist and "fellow-traveler" prewar Russophiles, those with extreme opinions about Russian foreign policy, pro or con, argue from the alleged existence or nonexistence of some recent "conversion" of Soviet leadership to an almost bourgeois respectability. At both extremes there are many who would agree that the Stalinist devil formerly had horns and a tail. The sanguine group now argue, however, that the horns and tail have been shed and that in its new manifestation Stalinism has sprouted wings and begun to sing with the angels. They now believe Stalinism is a wonderful thing—for Russia. They read into the Moscow and Teheran agreements all kinds of good omens for the future, only a few of which will prove accurate. The pessimistic group, on the basis of their belief that Stalinism remains evil, interpret every manifestation that Soviet policy is being conducted in the Soviet interest as fresh proof of their thesis. The recent formal decentralization of Soviet conduct of foreign affairs and army administration is immediately viewed by them as evidence that the whole of Slavic Europe is to be sovietized.

Two recent books on the Soviet Union, by William Henry Chamberlin [10] and David Dallin,[11] are performing a service in so far as they help to disabuse persons of a "pollyanna" view of the future of Russian foreign policy upon which they have been basing their hopes for a lasting peace. Such a peace, if it proves possible, will rest upon a demonstration to the satisfaction of each of the surviving powers of the first rank that the self-interest of each will be furthered by collaboration. One must assume a Russian foreign policy predicated upon motives neither more nor less moral than prewar motives. One must expect that, then as now, Russian policy will be based upon "Russia-first" considerations. There is some evidence that Russian interests may largely coincide with British and American interests, if the statesmen of all three powers apply intelligence to their efforts to further their respective national interests. This evidence needs to be evaluated before either sanguine or pessimistic expectations regarding the Western democracies are formulated.

Instead of being cynical about Soviet intentions, thoughtful and informed Americans will try first to understand Soviet objectives and to discover the extent to which these objectives can be reconciled with American objectives. Unless they make this effort they lessen the chance that the Soviet Union will choose to attain its foreign-policy ends by means which operate within a framework of Anglo-Soviet-American collaboration. For the Western democracies, whose foreign policies must of necessity reflect the main currents of public opinion, widespread public discussion and understanding of trends in Soviet policy provide the only firm basis for an efficient conduct of Anglo-Soviet and Soviet-American relations. We can afford the luxury neither of uncritical acceptance of every Soviet act nor of irresponsible denunciation of the system which produced the world's mightiest armies; nor can we afford the luxury of a diplomacy alternately influenced by these two extreme views.

Soviet co-operation in the task of maintaining peace is neither to be assumed nor to be rejected in advance. It is to be achieved. If the appetite of the Russian bear for more territory proves to be strictly limited, there is a basis for three-power collaboration, for Britain and America covet no land that the Soviet Union could possibly want. Is the U.S.S.R. within a decade or two going to make demands for new territories so extreme that collaboration is impossible? Several considerations point to a negative answer.

(1) The pitiless devastation of the Ukraine, of the other border republics in Europe, and of the territories occupied by Hitler's armies generally present the Soviet peoples with tasks of internal reconstruction of an unprecedented scope. They need time "to redecorate the interior of their own house." A costly reconstruction program does not preclude the possibility that the U.S.S.R. might, in the present war, drive a hard bargain with some of its Western neighbors, but, once hostilities have ceased, it probably will not want to wage war again soon. Renewed hostilities would delay reconstruction; this in turn would be as bad for the Soviet power position as it would be for the needs of its peoples. Its need for a breathing spell of peace and security should serve to moderate its program in Eastern Europe both now and later. To take too much now would be to increase the chance of attack later.

(2) There is another consideration that favors a stable rather than an extended western frontier. After a generation of privation and a period of planned sacrifice under the First Five-Year Plan, Russians tasted briefly, under the Second Five-Year Plan, the fruits of long sacrifice, in the form of greatly increased

production of consumers' goods. As the menace of the fascist powers grew more threatening, sacrifice again became the order of the day. The country transformed itself into a great arsenal. The unprecedented hardships of the war itself are only a climax of sacrifice to a people who must long for peace and prosperity.

(3) The mineral wealth of the Asiatic border republics has made possible an eastward movement of the U.S.S.R.'s economic center of gravity. The economic need to have factories built close to the raw material-producing areas, the political need to transform the backward border peoples into devoted and skilled citizens, and the military need to have relatively self-sufficient industrial areas located well away from the western frontier, all combined to make this eastward movement desirable.[12] The industrial enterprises hurriedly evacuated behind the Urals under pressure of war reinforced this tendency. Factories will, of course, be rebuilt in the devastated areas, but the demonstrated effectiveness of a grand strategy of defense means that territorial outposts deep in Europe may be regarded as strategic liabilities and very probably will not be regarded as strategic assets.

(4) In any case the effectiveness of the Soviet strategy of defense in depth depends in part upon the maintenance of an active guerrilla warfare behind the enemy lines and in part upon the countless individual deeds of heroism of an army fighting to defend its homes and to hurl back the fascist invaders. Unless, therefore, further Soviet territorial expansion should come as a result of a genuine demand from the masses of the peoples to be sovietized, it would not add greatly to the effectiveness of a defense in depth.*

(5) Communist ideology and national patriotism have combined to produce unity of effort in the present war. This unity

---

* The specific strategic advantages won by the incorporation of the three tiny Baltic states and the revision of the Finnish frontiers on the Karelian Isthmus outweighed considerations of genuine mass demand for bolshevization.

would be destroyed by further violent annexations. A cynical leadership might be tempted to divert the people's demand for bread by new adventures in foreign policy, but a whole generation of Russians has been indoctrinated in the "socialism in one country" doctrine. They would have difficulty in understanding how territorial expansion would further the mass distribution of goods and services. Those who are anxious to promote communism on a world-wide basis might be especially skeptical of the efficacy of bolshevization by the sword. Relatively small accretions to Soviet territory would be won at the cost of widespread support in the war on the world-wide ideological front. Even the short war of 1939-40 against Finland did grave damage to the cause of world-wide communism.*

(6) One technique by which the Soviet Union is consolidating its leadership in Eastern Europe is by appealing to Pan-Slav sentiments in that area. Its self-appointed role as protector of Slavic peoples could hardly be maintained if it deprived some of them of their national independence. The incorporation of the Baltic states, the Polish Ukraine, and Bessarabia into the Soviet Union all have historic justifications which could not apply to other Slavic areas.

(7) The events leading up to Russian participation in the Second World War suggest that neither Party nor Army leaders were eager to initiate hostilities. The Molotov-von Ribbentrop negotiation of a nonaggression pact in August, 1939, was certainly no contribution to the maintenance of peace, but it was an indication of the Soviet Union's desire to avoid war at almost any price.

(8) Even if Germany could be bolshevized, there are good reasons why this would not be welcome in Moscow. At present

---

* D. J. Dallin, *Russia and Postwar Europe*, New Haven, Yale University Press, 1943, pp. 18-48, assembles evidence of an inner conflict between the nationalist Red Army leaders and the old-time Communist party ideologues. However this struggle is resolved, it suggests the disunity which expansion either by conquest or by instigated revolution would produce.

the Moscow leadership is the single radiating center of communist policy and revolutionary propaganda. This leadership possesses a monopoly of insight as to the correct interpretation of the party line. No matter what forms of legal decentralization are accomplished by successive revisions of the Soviet Constitution, a real centralization of decision-making is guaranteed by the present organization of the Party. If an advanced industrial state with a highly literate and skilled population should be incorporated into the Union of Soviet Socialist Republics, there would be not one but two radiating centers of policy-making. Homogeneity of policy would be most difficult to achieve. As a major instrument of Soviet diplomacy, the Communist party will certainly be active in postwar Germany; but its role may be to work within the framework of the type of parliamentary regime which the July, 1943, Manifesto of the Moscow-sponsored National Committee of Free Germany envisioned for a leftist-liberal program.[13]

(9) A document of importance for Poland analogous to that of the Free German Manifesto for Germany is the "Declaration of Principle" adopted in Moscow by the Union of Polish Patriots in June, 1943.[14] This organization was created under Soviet auspices to provide an organizing nucleus for exiled Poles separate from that of the government-in-exile in London. It was the predecessor of the Polish National Council. While the declaration serves notice to the Western world that the Soviet Union strives for hegemony in the Eastern European tier of states along its borders, it also gives assurance that formal incorporation of great new areas into the Soviet Union is not contemplated.*

(10) There is another bit of evidence whose importance is subject to less doubt than its interpretation. This is the approaching enormous expansion of Soviet population during the next generation, both absolutely and in relation to the rest of

* Cf. *infra*, pp. 116-18, for a more complete discussion of the program of the Union of Polish Patriots.

Europe. Professor Frank Notestein and the Office of Population Research at Princeton University which he directs have pioneered in the demographic analysis which makes such a prediction possible.[15] On the assumptions of (a) no war losses and (b) no international migration, he has shown that the best estimate of Soviet population in 1970 is an increase from a 1940 figure of approximately 175,000,000 to about 250,000,000. Europe west of the U.S.S.R. would increase from about 400,000,000 to something less than 420,000,000.[16] Stating the same matter differently, the Soviet population will rise from 44 per cent of that of the rest of Europe to 60 per cent. Even if war losses make necessary some revision downward of these figures, the fact that both non-Russian Europe and the Soviet Union are experiencing such losses means that the ratios would not be altered substantially. Even more favorable from the point of view of the Soviet power position are the trends with respect to composition of the population by age groups. A rapidly expanding population has a large proportion of young men. A population whose rate of increase is leveling off is one which is aging rapidly. Thus in the fighting age groups the percentage of Russian to other European population will rise to much more than 60 per cent. By 1970, on the basis of these same figures, the Soviet Union would have 43.3 million men in the age group from fifteen to thirty-four years of age—as large a number as the next seven sources of manpower in Europe combined, viz., Germany, the United Kingdom, Italy, France, Poland, Spain, and Roumania.[17]

The Soviet Union has, therefore, no reason to involve itself in a preventive war when its own position is improving so rapidly with the passage of time. Only if the political consolidation of Europe under anti-Soviet auspices west of the Soviet Union were imminent would there be a Soviet interest in "preventive" expansion at the risk of general war. The population data therefore offer some assurance that the three super-powers will have at least a generation to collaborate amicably to promote general security and to discover a mutually satisfactory way of organizing Europe. At the same time these data offer a warning that there will be a day when the Anglo-American bargaining power will be less, that the time for establishing a collaborative pattern is now.

Tentatively, one may conclude that the Soviet Union will prefer greater security to additional territory. In certain cases, however, it will regard territory as essential to security.

To what extent do actual steps in Soviet foreign policy support the expectation that its territorial demands will be moderate? Some of them serve notice that Soviet collaboration in the postwar world is not to be taken for granted. By its continued second-front agitation, by publicizing such sensational "rumors" as the *Pravda* report of January 17, 1944, that von Ribbentrop and two prominent British personalities had been discussing peace terms, and by independent steps in policy such as the recognition of the Badoglio regime, the way has been kept open for Soviet leadership to denounce its present partners. A new departure in foreign policy would appear explicable to the Soviet masses by reference to these earlier evidences of lack of confidence. On the other side are steps clearly designed to show that the Soviet Union envisions the possibility of postwar collaboration with the Western powers. Most notable of these are the abolition of the Communist International, and the signing in 1943 of the Moscow and Teheran Declarations. There are also promising indications of a conciliatory attitude in the relatively mild peace terms offered Finland, in the agreements to preserve the independence of Iran, and in the statement which Soviet Foreign Commissar Molotov made at the time Red Army forces first crossed the boundary separating Bessarabia from Roumania proper. He announced that "the Soviet government declares that it does not pursue any aims of acquiring any part of the Roumanian territory or changing the existing social structure of Roumania, and that the entry of Soviet troops into Roumanian territory was caused exclusively by military necessity and by the continued resistance of troops of the enemy." [18] There can be little question that American and British opinion now wants very much to see postwar co-operation among the greatest powers, but it may be difficult to convince the naturally suspicious Soviet leaders that this desire will continue. Meanwhile, their foreign policy remains ambiguous, and each new Soviet step which has foreign policy implications is subjected to as many interpretations as there are interpreters. Positive evidence of Soviet intentions is inconclusive. One can, however, conclude that the door has not yet been closed to peace-time collaboration with Great Britain and the United States.

VI. The Price of Collaboration and the Consequences of Noncollaboration

> *Two dominant and mutually antagonistic poles of attraction have come into existence,* . . . *Britain-America is attractive in virtue of its wealth, for in this quarter loans are obtainable. The Soviet Union is attractive in virtue of its revolutionary experience.* . . .
>
> STALIN, in a speech at the Fourteenth Congress of the Communist Party, 1925.

IF Soviet leaders have not yet fully committed their country to postwar collaboration with the Western super-powers, it is because they do not yet know what price the Western powers are prepared to pay for such collaboration. The Soviet government may be very sure that it will not again be treated as a pariah and excluded from important international conferences as it was in the period from Versailles to Munich; but it probably seeks a great deal more than simply being welcomed into the inner circle of the decision-making powers. It has interests in Eastern and Central Europe which it will want its allies in war to recognize in the peace that follows. How extensive will be Soviet minimum requirements in this area is a matter of conjecture; but Britain and America must know how high a price they will have to pay for collaboration before they can decide whether or not to pay it.

The first installment is recognition of the 1939-41 additions to Soviet territory. Although Moscow has asserted its willingness to negotiate with a friendly Poland the frontiers between Poland and the border republics of the Soviet Union, it has never intimated that it would withdraw from non-Polish-speaking areas. The continued references in public speeches and in the official press to the newly added border republics as exact co-equals of the older republics demonstrate that the Soviet position is not open to reconsideration. The recent elevation of the constituent republics to a position entitling them to separate representation in foreign affairs may offer Britain and America an opportunity to concede the "independence" of the Baltic republics.*

The formal stamp of finality was put on the expansions of 1939-41 by the plebiscites and subsequent formal incorporation of the territories into the U.S.S.R. No great state may be expected to admit that its plebiscites were fraudulent. Replies to diplomatic notes attempting to reopen the question will certainly be brief and probably curt. Unless one has already decided that collaboration with Russia is impossible or undesirable, there is little point in raising this question.

Recognition of the pre-June, 1941, *faits accomplis* is not of course sufficient to guarantee amicable collaboration, for the U.S.S.R. has other plans which its Western partners will be asked to approve. The Soviet Union will want recognition of its right to a friendly regime in countries adjacent to its borders with the characteristics of "friendliness" determined in Moscow. This is the second installment which the British and American allies are being asked to pay as the price of collaboration. To understand why this demand is being put forward it is neces-

---

* Joachim Joesten, *What Russia Wants*, New York, Duell, Sloan and Pearce, 1944, Chapters IV-VI, has attempted to make such a concession palatable by assembling the very considerable evidence that the Soviet Union was provoked into action by fascist influences in Finland, the Baltic states, Poland, and Roumania.

sary to go back to the Soviet Union's Winter War with Finland in 1939-40.

Max Werner has described this war as the war that nobody won.[1] Soviet Russia's military victory was achieved at the price of a blot on her reputation for acting in good faith. By no conceivable interpretation of the Russo-Finnish Pact of Nonaggression of January 21, 1932, or the Convention for the Definition of Aggression which became binding on both by Finland's adherence, July 22, 1933, could the Soviet invasion of Finnish territory on November 30, 1939, be justified. The subsequent participation of Finland in Hitler's Russian adventure has seemed to many to have proved the need for the Soviet action, but the U.S.S.R.'s task of convincing its nearest neighbors of its peaceful intentions, so that they will not seek support from some other great power, has become even more difficult than before. It is this difficulty which makes it so necessary for the U.S.S.R. to bring its great influence to bear on the composition of its neighbors' governments.

Such intervention, especially when it occurs on a scale that precludes similar pressure from Britain or America, arouses distrust among the Western powers as to the Soviet Union's ultimate territorial ambitions. One clue to Soviet intentions in this matter, the Declaration of Principles of the Union of Polish Patriots, has already been mentioned. This document develops, as an alternative to territorial claims, the Soviet claim to a "friendly" regime in neighboring states. To accept this claim gracefully the Western allies will have to believe in the good faith and essential reasonableness of the Russians. To accept it with obvious reluctance might be to destroy the value of the concession, for it would reinforce Soviet convictions as to the necessity of the concession. This second installment is sometimes described as recognition of a special Soviet security sphere.

Will there be a third installment? Specifically, do the U.S.S.R. or the Western allies have plans for the future of Germany which the other would have difficulty in accepting?

A direct answer to this question will be postponed until it can be placed in a proper frame of reference.*

Beyond Germany to the West there will be no special price to pay for Soviet collaboration. In this fourth area, Soviet diplomacy will operate through normal channels. When diplomatic advantage can be taken of Anglo-American steps or missteps it will be taken. Thus, one of the most astute of Soviet negotiators, Andrei Vyshinsky, was sent to sit with the Allied Commission at Algiers. A determined effort was made to enlist the good will of the De Gaullist government, an effort which contrasted with the somewhat frigid, hesitant, and limited recognition accorded it by the United States and Great Britain. The Soviet government may one day need a friend in Western Europe, and here was an inexpensive way of making friends.

In this fourth zone and in a fifth, the home territories of the Western super-powers, the Soviet government has taken steps to remove charges of ideological intervention from the arena of diplomatic controversy. The Soviet Union has in the past sometimes been charged with pursuing a dual diplomacy. When normal diplomacy has failed, the Communist International has sometimes provoked agitation in the recalcitrant country. The abolition of that organization does not mean that Communists will cease to regard the Soviet Union as their second fatherland. It does mean that national legislation in Western Europe and in Britain and America restricting Communist activity will cause no diplomatic impasse between Moscow and the West.

The outlines of Soviet security policy now begin to emerge. Instead of viewing the frontiers between the Soviet and non-Soviet worlds as a thin line, Soviet leaders seem to be developing a conception of a "belt of frontiers." [2] Moving outward from Moscow one passes through zones in which Soviet aspirations for hegemony progressively diminish. It is in Europe that these

* Cf. *infra*, Chapter VII.

zones are most highly differentiated, perhaps because this populous and industrially powerful continent separating the Western powers from the Soviet Union is the chief problem-area in present-day world politics.

At the heart of the Soviet world is the R.S.F.S.R. Here, Communist doctrine and Great Russian nationality combine. Still within the formal limits of the U.S.S.R., as of June, 1941, is a belt of border nationalities, consisting of the fifteen other constituent republics of the Soviet Union. These republics have had their formal equality with the gigantic R.S.F.S.R. emphasized by the formal allocation to them in 1944 of responsibilities in foreign affairs and defense. It was in this belt that the 1939-41 expansions took place. Adjacent to the legal frontiers of the U.S.S.R. is a Soviet security belt in which Moscow will insist on a regime friendly to the Soviet government and allied to no other great power. Beyond the belt of friendly regimes is Germany. Here Allied pressure from the West and Soviet pressure from the East will reach some type of equilibrium.* In the next belt are the states whose political orientation will be more toward the British and American power-nucleus. Here one may expect Soviet diplomacy to limit itself to inhibiting as far as practicable the complete consolidation of these areas into an aggressive anti-Soviet coalition. The British and American centers of power complete this strategic map of the world of the super-powers.

This is a conception of security spheres. It does not, as many assert, preclude Anglo-Russian-American collaboration. Europe has long been accustomed to British insistence that the Low Countries not become bases for hostile action and to the idea

* China will in certain instances present an analogous problem in the Far East. It will be the area in which Soviet and Anglo-American power reach equilibrium, but, unlike Germany, it is in this generation a "low-pressure" power area. Germany is in our time strong and will be weak only so long as the present war coalition is determined in peace time to keep it so. If the Soviet Union formally enters the Far Eastern war, Japan also would belong in this fourth category.

of the Caribbean Sea as practically an inland water of the United States. What will inhibit collaboration is Soviet insistence on the one hand or Anglo-American insistence on the other on a security sphere so extensive and so complete that it might later be used as a base for further and possibly unlimited expansion. There is no necessity to choose between security spheres and collaboration. The final settlement will contain elements of each.

Germany cannot, of course, be included in the security sphere of either the Eastern or the Western power-nuclei without destroying the possibility of three-power collaboration. For with Germany incorporated in either bloc the chief threat to the security of the other would come from the bloc including Germany. On the other hand, were Germany soon again to be permitted to achieve status as an independent power-nucleus of the first magnitude, the whole pattern of postwar politics as envisioned in Moscow and Washington would break down. A distribution of power similar to that of the 1930's and equally ominous would prevail. Thus, the three surviving greatest powers will pay a heavy penalty for failure to agree on the problem of Germany. It is this which makes it a prerequisite of peace that a pattern of collaboration supplement a pattern of security spheres.

This discussion of Soviet collaboration with the West has so far been posited on the assumption that the Western democracies and the Soviet Union will constitute the poles of world politics. This does not necessarily mean that they will be polar *opposites* in the postwar world. To describe completely the functioning of a bipolar power system one must describe the circumstances under which it will transform itself into a system with a greater or lesser number of poles. A "no-pole" or, what may be very much the same, a "many-pole" system has already been ruled out in the first chapter, at least for our own time. A "tripolar" system is not, however, beyond the realm of possibility. The assumption of bipolarity therefore needs to be explored, particularly if there is a possibility that Germany constitutes a potential third pole. This circumstance is at once perilous and hopeful. It is perilous because a rearmed Germany could again plunge the world into war; it is hopeful because, as we shall see, it gives both Moscow and the West a very great incentive to agree on the solution of the German problem.

When one says that the central fact about the international politics of the next generation is that the Anglo-American combination and the Soviet Union will be the two strongest aggregations of power, he seems to imply that the chief threat to world peace in our children's time will be the tendency for political opponents to define their positions primarily with respect to their agreement or disagreement with Washington or Moscow. If these two capitals are in fact the centers around which potentially hostile forces tend to gather, the most probable line-up in a third world war, if that event should unhappily occur, should now be foreseeable. The high politics of our time would hold few major mysteries for the man who could prove that these were the poles of political discord. His proof, however, would have to include demonstrations that the two strongest powers were necessarily bound to oppose each other and that there were only two such centers of power.

It has already been argued that the Soviet and the Western-democratic aggregations of power are not necessarily bound to oppose each other for the following reasons: (1) they present no direct threat to each other since their geographic separation gives each ample opportunity to take countermeasures in case the other should strive for world hegemony; (2) each can generate maximum power only when it has been attacked; (3) a war between them would be long drawn out, inconclusive, and destructive of the material and moral accomplishments of civilization to a degree unparalleled even in the first two world wars. It will now be further argued that failure to consider the possible emergence of a third, German, nucleus of opposition and to take adequate steps to prevent such an emergence ignores the most dangerous threat to peace in the coming generation.

There can of course be but two sides in a war which has become global in extent and total in intensity, but, except in periods of general war, the organization of the world around two poles of discord has rarely been clearly observed. Even during the decade before 1939, when thoughtful observers everywhere were predicting a new world conflagration, there were not two but three poles to which potentially hostile forces gravitated.* The United States was not one of the three, nor was it one of the original belligerents, and the Soviet Union was also a non-belligerent when war finally came. In both world wars the powers around which coalitions were ultimately formed were Great Britain and Germany. The two now judged to be "strongest," after a period of standing aloof, entered the Second World War but entered it on the same side. Had a forecast been based primarily upon a correct estimate and comparison of Soviet and American war potentials, it might have been misleading. The two were not polar opposites either in the peace preceding the war or in the war itself.

It was not by mutually skillful management and attitudes of calculated conciliation that the giants of the Old World and of the New avoided conflict with each other. On the contrary, their leaders exchanged insults and engaged in diplomatic and military activities which in another context might well have precipitated war. It may after this war take more skill to avoid hostilities.

The danger is probably not so much that either power will deliberately and directly seek conflict with the other, since the evidence is so clear that such a conflict would be a catastrophe

---

* On the essential ambiguity of a triangle situation, see Sigmund Neumann, *Permanent Revolution*, New York, Harpers, 1942, pp. 284 ff. In the 1930's there were three poles not only from a military but from an ideological point of view. The triangle—Britain-France, Germany, and the Soviet Union—was paralleled by the triangle—democracy, fascism, and communism.

to both, in terms of the values which each pursues. Victory over the other, even if it could be attained, and that is itself doubtful, would involve the sacrifice of other values for the loss of which military victory would hardly compensate. The greater danger is that they will be drawn into a third world war *indirectly* or *reluctantly*—indirectly by finding themselves in a conflict which is not at first a Soviet-American war, or reluctantly by the leadership in one country coming to be convinced that conflict with the other is "inevitable."

The "indirect" possibility is in turn two-fold, since in being drawn into a war which started between another pair of powers, they might be drawn in, either on the same or on opposite sides, through failure to identify in time the true poles of conflict and to take necessary preventive action. Such a failure would result from an acceptance, perhaps unnecessarily, of the thesis that the Soviet Union and the Anglo-American groups of powers are polar opposites. The "reluctant" possibility also presupposes an acceptance of this thesis of bipolarity, and it should be noted that the thesis would become true simply by being believed.

It follows that if Soviet and Anglo-American leaders are anxious to avoid unnecessary war, they will be jointly interested in stabilizing Western Europe and Eastern Asia on a basis which will permit the rise of no new poles of aggressive action. They will not accept the thesis that they are fated to be polar opposites in the next global conflict until all other possibilities have been eliminated.

In one respect the prospects for such a conflict have been increased by the events since 1941. American military strength was largely undeveloped. Soviet military strength was greatly underestimated both in the camp of the fascists and in that of the Western democracies. Thus, although the public vocabulary of politicians in both the Soviet Union and the United States frequently located the world capital of the chief competing ideology in the other, the leaders of neither nation really believed that the other was its immediate, chief enemy. Hitler's aggressions instead made the two states allies. The course of the Second World War has, however, demonstrated the true strength of both aggregations of power. It will therefore be a commonplace after this war to speak of the United States and the Soviet Union as the "Big Two" whose falling-out will be the curtain raiser for the Third World War.

The destruction of German military might will further bring into relief the very great strength of the surviving world powers. Victorious generals and admirals have a way of casting a speculative eye upon their partners in victory in order to discover their probable opponents in the next war. In their long-range thinking, they may be preoccupied less with Germany than with each other. They, and the civilian policy-makers whom they advise, may develop a habit of thinking of the Second World War as a possible preliminary to the final bout in which the opposing forces of Soviet Russia and an Anglo-American bloc, of communism and free enterprise, of dictatorship and democracy, are locked in mortal conflict.

There is a further circumstance of an apparently menacing nature, the coming sharp expansion of Soviet population and of Soviet power in the course of the next generation. From the Soviet point of view, this is a circumstance which favors a conciliatory policy in the immediate postwar period. From the point of view of the noncommunist world, an exactly opposite interpretation is possible. It might be argued that the Soviet power-nucleus should be broken up while there is yet time.

Does this new accession of Soviet power necessarily constitute a threat to the United States and Great Britain? To speak of military strength as if it were some absolute phenomenon whose increase and decrease can be described in statistical terms is to distract attention from facts which determine whether that strength menaces some other state. If military power could be accurately measured and applied with equal efficiency at any point upon the earth's surface, then a drastic and continuing improvement in the Soviet Union's potential or actual military position would certainly cause many Americans the most serious misgivings. Under such circumstances the extrapolation of present trends would indicate that at a certain future date the Soviet Union would become "stronger" than an Anglo-American combination. Americans might be tempted to assume that Russian increase of power would have to be countered "before it is too late." Such an assumption would find ready acceptance among those who feel that mass discontent with special-privilege groups might be diverted if national energies could be organized around the task of checking Soviet Russia. The prospects for avoiding the organization of the world into two hostile armed camps would apparently be slight. The relatively conciliatory gestures of a Soviet Russia which was confident that it could afford to wait would be rejected, and a fresh descent into global war would not be long delayed.

We know, however, that "power" is not capable of being described in purely quantitative terms. It has to be described in terms which include estimates of the military strength of the opponent or combination of opponents against whom it is to be used; the objectives for which the power is to be used; the capacity to attract allies as the struggle proceeds favorably or unfavorably; the period during which maximum power can be maintained; the interval before maximum strength is reached; and its effectiveness when used on one's own territory, in that of the chief enemy, or in various other areas. What may be an element of strength when dealing with one opponent may be of no importance or even an element of weakness in dealing with another. Thus, the Axis powers may have been admirably organized for the winning of short wars but inadequate against the inherently greater strength of their opponents.

The pressure which either the Soviet Union or the Western powers can bring to bear upon the other in its main centers of power is surely much less than is implied by the statement that the two are the strongest forces in the world. Not only are the points of direct contact few and inaccessible but the centers are widely separated. The armed power of each can be effectively carried only part of the way to the other. American control over the seaward approaches to the New World will in any foreseeable future render a transoceanic operation by the Soviet Union impossible. The massive superiority of its land army should on the other hand discourage the Western powers from attempting a large-scale amphibious operation against hostile shores controlled by the Red Army.

What then are the prospects for a war between the Soviet eastern power-nucleus and the Anglo-American western aggregation? If either were to allow the other to consolidate the rimland of the Eurasian land mass under its control, it would also have permitted its own power position *vis-à-vis* the other to be irretrievably damaged.[3] Although a third world war is thus not likely to *start* as a Soviet-Anglo-American war, an attempt by either at sole hegemony in non-Russian Europe or Asia would almost certainly *finish* as a Soviet-Anglo-American war. This is almost the sole condition under which the two powers would become polar opposites in a world war.

A more immediate risk, however, is a bid for sole hegemony in the rimland which may come from some power or combination of powers within the rimland area. Germany is almost the only conceivable nucleus of such a power combination. If it should make such a bid, there would be a situation not unlike that prevailing in the thirties during which there were three great aggregations of power organized around three centers with three rival ideologies, each of which reviled the other two. Ideological differences reinforced traditional rivalries, and an inherently unstable European power structure was in an especially precarious position. Instability was accompanied by unpredictability, for this tripolar—Anglo-American, German, Soviet—organization of power could resolve itself into an alignment of two polar opposites only with the outbreak of general war.

It was extremely unlikely that the Second World War would start as a struggle between the Soviet Union and the Western democracies. Both the Soviet Union and the Anglo-French combination were strongly tempted to stand aloof while Germany and the other fought an indecisive war. It was only certain that *if* there were to be war, Germany would be an early and prominent participant. Will Germany again be one of the great-state poles of conflict around which forces working for a fresh trial by battle will gather? It is within the power of the three surviving super-powers, if they act together, to prevent such an eventuality.

They must guard against a bid from Germany for hegemony in Europe not in 1950 but after 1960. Global wars do not follow one another within a single decade. A prostrate Germany and a vigilant victorious coalition will remove the threat temporarily from that quarter. There is no difficult short-run problem. In the "middle run," however, there may be some danger. The mid-fifties will see a temporary increase in those age groups in the population between fifteen and thirty-four years of age, an increase which reflects the sharp but temporary increase in the German birth rate after 1933.[4] By this time the German industrial plant will have been largely reconstructed, and relaxation of controls over and inspection of German arms may well have set in. If one assumes, as one must, that dreams of imperial aggrandizement may again animate German leadership and again strike a responsive chord in the German "followership," then the period of relative improvement in Germany's power position would be a period of maximum danger for Germany's neighbors. The danger would of course be increased if the United Nations are unskillful in their solution of the German problem during the first few postwar years.

In the Russo-German relationship, the "middle-run" considerations may not seem so important. Germany will inevitably fall behind the Soviet Union in pig-iron production and even farther behind in population. Its long-run power position *vis-à-vis* the Soviet Union will worsen. The Russian population backlog will be so great that the Soviet leaders might contemplate minor and temporary improvements in the German demographic pattern without trepidation. Furthermore, Soviet policy does not, if the present regimented social organization persists, have to reckon with a public opinion which has lost its will to enforce upon Germany a Carthaginian peace.

For the Western powers who are themselves experiencing long-run shifts in their population patterns similar to those of Germany, the improvement in the German power position would seem more dangerous than for the Soviet Union. This may make more difficult the maintenance of a common Soviet-Anglo-American front against renewed German aggression. Soviet leaders may be tempted again to try to balance the world without their own state's being fully committed. A moderate increase in German strength might even be regarded as a healthy check upon a potentially anti-communist West.[5] With the consequent diminishing faith in Washington and London in the Soviet Union as a dependable partner in the coalition to enforce peace, the stage would be set for a second competitive appeasement of a reviving Germany.

The danger of such a course is obvious, for the German geographic position will still be such as to make a minimum of military power of maximum effect. The smaller powers of Europe may again refuse to stand firm against German revisionist demands until they are sure of support from both East and West. Ruling classes which are threatened by a rising mass discontent may again prefer to see their countries enslaved by a German enemy than saved by a Soviet friend. All this points to Germany's becoming a third power-nucleus around which will gather forces opposed to the settlement made after this war.

The Third World War can, if it starts, begin either as a war between Germany and the West (with an Anglo-American combination replacing the Anglo-French as the nucleus) or as a war between Germany and the Soviet Union (although German experience with the Red Army may discourage an early repetition of that experience). It is difficult to imagine that war will start at all if the united front against Germany (or any other aggressor) is maintained by the surviving great-power victors.

What bearing does this discussion have upon the assumption that the Western powers and the Soviet Union will be polar opposites? Such an opposition is not impossible, and its possibility should serve as a primary incentive for both Moscow and Washington to see that it does not happen. The risks of Soviet-Anglo-American co-operation are slight, especially when viewed in relation to the risks attendant upon possible fresh emergence of a German power-nucleus and the treacherous tripolar pattern. It is this tripolar organization which is the real alternative in our own time to peace guaranteed by preponderant and co-ordinated Soviet-Anglo-American power.

As between the risk of acting as if the Soviet Union will be a trustworthy partner in maintaining peace and the risk of acting as if it will not, the lesser risk is clearly that based on expectation of Soviet good faith. Otherwise, United States policy will facilitate the reconstitution of German power and the rebuilding of *Festung Europa* which we are just now laboriously and painfully dismantling. It would further make it possible for an insecure Soviet leadership to justify postponing for one more generation the mass distribution of consumers' goods and to return to the upbuilding of gigantic armed power and to a program of preventive annexation in Europe and ideological intervention throughout the world. If we assume faith in the motives and integrity of the Soviet government, there is a good chance of agreement upon a common program of Soviet-Anglo-American leadership in peace as in war. The three powers will of course not only have to agree to co-operate but also agree upon a specific program. The organization of postwar Europe and especially its German nucleus is the most pressing item on their agenda of collaboration. The most favorable omen for success in this task is the terrible penalty which the three powers and the world will pay if they fail.

PART FOUR

THE AGENDA OF COLLAB-
ORATION

VII. Germany and the New Europe

> *When the day comes for Germany to have a lamb's heart in her wolf's body, and for the will to peace to become the new way of the world—we shall need no federation whatsoever.*
>
> FRANS VAN CAUWELAERT, on "Dangers of a European Federation"

BRITAIN, the Soviet Union, and America cannot be expected to collaborate in a vacuum. The test of their capacity to cooperate will be in their agreement on the proper solution of a series of problems which will present themselves during and after the war. It is premature to prescribe detailed solutions to problems not yet clearly formulated. The advocate of three-power collaboration must nevertheless demonstrate that such collaboration is feasible. The condition of effective joint action is agreement upon certain basic objectives. Is there such agreement?

In a former age the powers of first rank were closely grouped within Europe but fought all over the world. In the present age the powers of first rank confront each other in every part of the world, but from their main centers of power look out at each other across Europe. This is the age of the peripheral powers. Instead of continental Europe's being the arbiter of the world's destiny, it has become the arena within which forces greater than itself will operate. It will be the chief, although not the exclusive, theater in which the drama of world politics will be played.*

It would be a mistake, however, to write as if Europe's role were the purely passive one of being the arena of conflict or co-operation of the great peripheral super-powers. Forces will not only be brought to bear upon Europe, but they will be welling up within it. A program which fails to assay the probable reactions of elements within Europe to the pressures brought to bear from without is unrealistic. Thus, programs which seek to achieve peace among the super-powers at the expense of the European community might conceivably achieve the integration of Europe under German (or even Franco-German) auspices. It is this integration which the civilized world is now pouring out its life blood to prevent. The terrible penalty which may be visited upon the victorious super-powers if they fail to collaborate in peace has been discussed. There will also be a penalty if they do collaborate but do so in a way which consolidates Europe against them. The task of the collaborating super-powers is therefore complicated. They must find a basis for common action which satisfies the legitimate needs of each; but a solution which is flagrantly unsatisfactory to large elements in Europe will be found to be "no solution."

Upon the promotion of what kind of new order in Europe could the three greatest of the postwar powers agree? Would this order be buttressed from within by the ungrudging support of politically decisive groups in various parts of Europe? These two questions must both be answered before one can draw up an agenda of three-power collaboration.

The statesmen of all three countries profess as their objectives peace based upon justice. Statesmen in all countries have professed similar objectives. If "justice" in fact meant the same thing to all men, armed conflict would never be necessary. As disputes occurred, the higher conception of justice would be

* British, American, and Soviet power will also converge in the Far East, the Middle East, and the Near East.

invoked to resolve the particular conflict. Both disputants would accept the indicated solution. Questions of power and prestige would not be raised. In the opposite situation, in which there is a total absence of moral consensus, *bellum omnium contra omnes* would be normal.

Neither extreme is likely to occur in the postwar world. With Germany and Japan struck from the list of powers of the first rank, some community of values among the surviving great powers is possible. Ideological differences, on the other hand, preclude the possibility of a complete identity of values as between the United States, the Soviet Union, and Great Britain.

Does this partial agreement on objectives furnish a basis upon which to reorder the world? The architects of the postwar world must work with the materials at hand. At the least they will find that the three super-powers do not envision the absorption of each other as immediate objectives of foreign policy. They can therefore afford to explore the possibility of working together. Nor does any one of the three place continuous enlargement of national territory at the top of its scheme of values. A coalition which heightened the security of each might thus be preferred to a diplomatic isolation in which each was thrown back exclusively upon its own resources. The stated objectives of all three societies can be more easily reached if each power is not continuously threatened by a power of something like equal stature, and if it is separated from the other super-powers by areas which are not potential bases of aggression.

The first general principle upon which the three may agree thus emerges. Since a united Europe would be a base with greater material and human resources than any one of the super-powers, there should be no consolidation of Europe under a single hegemony either by one of themselves or by a power within Europe.* Neither should Europe be divided among the

---

* Disunited, Western Europe's head start on the road to a declining population and an even more rapidly declining group of military age, together

super-powers with some line in Central Europe as their common frontier.

In any of these events the world of the super-powers would no longer exhibit the distinctive feature which is its most promising augury of an era of stability, the geographic separateness of the centers of greatest power. It would also no longer exhibit another feature which would facilitate the attainment of a stable political equilibrium, namely, a number of efficient small states.[1] These can act as makeweights in attaining stable equilibrium by associating themselves in particular cases with the forces of stability. Only great powers bent upon expansionist aggression could object to such a development, and the absorption by any one of them of its smaller neighbors would sound the alarm for a new coalition against aggression.

Simply to divide Europe between East and West not only would give a wholly undesirable inflexibility to the postwar power system but would in addition outrage the sensibilities of Europeans of all kinds. It might even lead them to think that perhaps after all Hitler had been right, that the "New Order" was a way to organize Europe against the barbarians from without. Lacking such a provocation the possibility that Europe will spontaneously coalesce into a single political unit is slight.[2] Adolf Hitler has destroyed whatever enthusiasm for Pan-Europa may have existed. Since Germany is the only nucleus within Europe around which forcible consolidation could take place, the first problem is to discover the strategic controls which would render the fresh rise of an expansionist Germany impossible.

Whatever scheme is chosen, it will be implemented only if there is a continuing will on the part of all the major victors to enforce the terms of peace upon Germany in so far as they relate to the reduction of German power. Unless both Great

with the enormous destruction of its painfully accumulated capital wealth, would seem to guarantee this area's relative passivity in the international politics of the coming years.

Britain and Soviet Russia support policies designed to prevent the reconstruction of German power, the policy cannot be successful.

This conclusion leads one back, by a process of circular reasoning, to the question whether the super-powers will in fact find it possible to agree on general objectives, for it is chiefly fear of each other which would permit the vigilance of Britain and the Soviet Union in the matter of enforcing peace terms upon Germany to be relaxed. The extent of Britain's willingness to keep its commitments in Europe up to a level adequate to enforce security also depends on the continuing support of the United States. Given three-power agreement, the problem of disarming Germany via the use of strategic controls and vigilant inspection is a technical problem for which a solution will be found.

A similar observation may be made with respect to all the political "defenses in depth" which may be erected against a recrudescent German power.* The first line of defense, unilateral disarmament, with its objective of keeping Germany from starting again on a program of expansion, may be reinforced by a second line, an alliance designed to stop Germany quickly if it ever does launch a new attack on the European order. The Anglo-Soviet twenty-year defensive alliance of May 26, 1942, is the essential core of such a continuing coalition.

By building around an Anglo-Soviet agreement an alliance system to keep Germany in check, one mistake made in the Locarno Pact has been avoided. By the terms of that agreement Germany voluntarily agreed to arrangements which seemed to enhance British, French, and Belgian security along her western borders, while making no corresponding arrangements for her eastern borders. This omission was interpreted in

* Cf. Arnold Wolfers, *Britain and France between Two Wars*, New York, Harcourt, Brace, 1940, Chapter X. "*L'organisation de la paix*," in terms of which he describes the French quest for security, is a conception parallel to the political "defenses in depth" discussed *infra*.

various German circles as an invitation to question the *status quo* in the East. When Britain and France accepted Nazi remilitarization of the Rhineland in direct violation of the Locarno Pact, they destroyed the last chance that France could render effective aid to her small-power allies in Eastern Europe. From that time forward there could be security neither in the East nor in the West. The diplomatic catastrophe of Munich was the final demonstration of the indivisibility of the European security problem.

The super-powers may want to take special steps to consolidate their own security spheres in Europe, but they must not do it by attempting to channel German aggression into someone's else security sphere. Only so long as they have a common policy toward Germany can they effectively resist this temptation.

The first and second lines of defense against aggression will be erected specifically against Germany because for at least a generation there can be no comparable threat to all three of the super-powers from any other power. This is only partly because of an inherent defect in German culture and not at all, of course, because of any defect in the biological heritage. There are few states of very great power and the three greatest are assumed to be nonexpansionist; therefore, the number of remaining potential initiators of general war is small. In Europe even a prostrate Germany is, at the present stage of history, the greatest threat.

The general security organization which is to take action against an "aggressor" is in fact therefore a third line of defense against Germany. Its function is to mobilize against the aggressor a larger number of states than the more specific commitments could mobilize, in the event aggression is not stopped quickly and spreads into general war. It would not prevent German rearmament, and it could not act quickly and decisively in a crisis; but it could broaden the coalition against a new aggressor and thus aid in the aggressor's ultimate defeat. It must be remembered, however, that a general security organization could survive the crisis of restraining German aggression only if it had the active support of all three super-powers.

At all three stages, therefore, the control of German expansionist tendencies depends upon a tripartite consensus as to the future of Germany and of Europe. Prevention of German aggression of itself would achieve the first objective upon which the super-powers may be expected to agree, the nonconsolidation of Europe under a single hegemony.

This does not mean a program of cynically keeping Europe disunited so that by promoting discord within Europe the peripheral powers may protect themselves. They have, on the contrary, the greatest interest in preventing strife in non-Russian Europe, an interest which is only exceeded by their interest in preventing strife among themselves or between a consolidated Europe and themselves. There is a unity which they must seek to promote in Europe, and it is a unity for which Europe is striving. It is, however, a unity of ideals rather than of allegiance to a common master. The real difficulty with the federation of Europe, from the point of view of many Europeans, is that "Europe" is not a natural unit for organization.[3] As Van Cauwelaert, a Belgian, has written, "the sea has freer and wider vistas than the land. We are not simply a Belgian frontier province on a continent. We are, like Holland, a door that opens wide upon the ocean. . . . The distance between Belgium and America, counted in cost of transportation, is less than that between Brussels and Sofia. It is less, too, in the domain of thought and popular tradition. Our international orientation should be maritime and not continental, Atlantic and not European."[4]

What Europe needs and requires is not a unity of political or economic organization but a unity of general security and a freedom of autonomous development for large and small nations alike. It will come from the elimination everywhere in Europe of those types of political behavior which make men desire to dominate and exploit and which are therefore incompatible with any universal conception of the order and dignity of man.[5] Here is revealed the second principle upon which the super-powers may agree, the complete suppression of fascist tendencies in postwar European governments, in so far as it lies within their collective power to do so. The first, "anti-hegemony," principle may be described as directed against the regimentation of peoples; the second, "anti-fascist," principle, against regimentation of persons.

With respect to France, and the internal organization of the Low Countries and Norway, in what may be called the Anglo-American security sphere, there need be no disagreement between the Western powers and the Soviet Union. With democracy again functioning in these states, there is virtually no chance of their being used as bases for an anti-Anglo-American coalition. Thus, in this area the special Anglo-American security interest and the general Soviet-Anglo-American interest in antifascist government reinforce each other. All will want to see the complete restoration of democratic forms of government.

In what is beginning to be called the Soviet security sphere in Central and Eastern Europe, it may be more difficult for the three major powers to agree on the mutually acceptable antifascist principles upon which the governments of these areas are to be based. Moscow's elaborate demonstrations of good will toward the Czechoslovak government-in-exile of Eduard Beneš [6] and the equally clear manifestations of ill will toward the Polish government-in-exile as constituted at the beginning of 1944 * are positive and negative clues as to what constitutes the "friendly regimes" which the Soviet Union says it must have set up, for its own security, in the belt of states which divides it from Germany and Western Europe.

A document which is apparently important in revealing Moscow's preferences for the future Poland is the "Declaration of

* E.g., the rupture of diplomatic relations in April, 1943, and subsequent refusals to resume relations.

Principles" adopted by the Union of Polish Patriots in Moscow in June, 1943.[7] This organization was created in Moscow avowedly because of dissatisfaction with the Polish government in London. In this Declaration the U.S.S.R. is referred to as Poland's "only natural ally." There is a call for "a solid alliance after the war," for "political and economic cooperation" between Poland and Czechoslovakia, for "a democratic Poland, where the national interests are not subordinated to the interests of the governing," for agrarian reform and "a Poland freed of the rule of the country squires," for "an independent Poland . . . not . . . a pawn of foreign imperialism," for a Poland shorn of Ukrainian and White Russian areas but strengthened by the incorporation of Silesia and East Prussia, and for a Poland "in a position to assume the burden of joint responsibility for mounting a peaceful guard on the Oder so as to make a new German aggression impossible." Poland, and presumably the whole eastern tier of non-Russian states in Europe, are apparently to have a more intimate relationship with the Soviet Union than with Germany, but Soviet domination over Poland's external and internal affairs is not to be carried to the point of full incorporation.*

The territorial arrangements suggested are of interest at this point, because by uniting the Polish Ukraine with the Soviet Ukraine, and by adding to the new Poland East Prussia, large concentrations of great landed proprietors in both Germany and Poland, the German Junkers and the Polish "country squires," would be adversely affected. This, taken together with the separate mention of agrarian reform, suggests that the Soviet leaders would prefer a nation of small farmers on their borders. They

* There will also probably be in the Far East a Soviet security belt not formally incorporated in the Soviet Union but so supervised that it could not easily be used as a base for anti-Soviet operations. Great ingenuity has already been shown in inventing legal forms to express this relationship in Outer Mongolia and will be shown with respect to Manchuria and possibly Korea, but the forms will not necessarily be those used in Eastern Europe.

would seem to want in Poland a regime which would never permit the return to power of the Polish latifundia owners.

The program of the Union of Polish Patriots advocates in foreign affairs a Polish-Soviet alliance and in internal affairs a government whose class composition is not likely to be anti-Soviet. It thus guarantees a Poland which would not be a base for an anti-Soviet coalition.* Would it be a Poland whose government Great Britain and the United States might recognize as satisfying the general interest in anti-fascist democratic governments throughout Europe? No clear answer can be given, but it should be noted that a Polish government constituted as was the Czechoslovak government of Beneš before Munich would fulfill the requirements regarding internal reform. The present Czech government has shown that it is possible for a noncommunist regime to be on good terms simultaneously with Washington, London, and Moscow. If, therefore, the Soviet government demands regimes in Poland and in the rest of Eastern Europe no more radical than that of Beneš's Czechoslovak government, there should be little reason for Anglo-American protest.

Degree of anti-fascist democracy may not, however, be the point in dispute between Moscow and the West. The difficulty may instead be the extent of Soviet intervention in the internal politics of its neighbors. In more settled times it is difficult even for a great state to force modifications in the internal regimes of its small neighbors. At a time, however, when it is difficult to know how faithfully a government-in-exile reflects the wishes of its enslaved people and when the chain of constitutional legality which binds the exiled regime to its legitimate past is of dubious strength, the opportunities for a great neighbor to

* Parenthetically, one should note the very extreme Soviet suggestions for a Polish-German frontier on the Oder. Such a frontier would be a standing barrier to Polish-German friendship. Poland would be forced to retain the good will of the Soviet Union to protect itself against irredentist German pressures.

influence future regimes in the areas being liberated are great. The Polish National Council, for example, were it permitted to become the Polish government-in-exile which the Soviet Union recognizes, would have a tremendous advantage over its London competitor if it should be the regime to which the liberating Red Army were to hand over the government. What limit then can be set to Soviet dictation of the composition of the postwar Polish government? The British and American governments will not make war on the Soviet Union to prevent the creation of a near communist vassal Poland.

Two factors serve to limit the extent of Soviet intervention. The Soviet government prefers regimes in neighboring states which spontaneously support friendly collaboration with the Soviet Union. Involuntary sovietization or the use of puppet regimes might jeopardize spontaneous support. It might also hamper the spread of communist ideology since the Soviet Union could then be charged with imperialistic expansion. Furthermore, the Soviet Union would have to abandon use of the slogans of Pan-Slavism and liberation nationalism. A Soviet *Lebensraum* and a Soviet "New Order" would be little more popular than their Nazi predecessors.

In the second place, the less moderation shown in dealing with its smaller Eastern neighbors, the less effective would be the possible collaboration with the Western democracies. Britain and America can no more by direct action prevent the Soviet Union from being its own judge as to what constitutes a friendly, anti-fascist regime in Eastern Europe than Britain or the Soviet Union could prevent the United States from making a fresh landing of marines in Nicaragua.

The United States would pay a heavy penalty for unprovoked intervention in a Latin American state, since its good neighbor policy would be destroyed and its moral authority throughout the world lessened. Similarly, the Soviet Union will be judged at the bar of democratic world opinion; and if its influence in Eastern Europe is misused, it too will pay a high price.

British and American diplomats can only urge upon the Soviet government a course of moderation, i.e., urge upon it the advantages of a true good neighbor policy within the zone of its paramount interest. Their governments can set an example for such moderation by the scrupulous respect which they show for the independence of the smaller countries within their own power orbits. They can further set an example by the care with which they make sure that loans for relief and rehabilitation and long-term reconstruction in the Soviet power orbit are devoid of anti-democratic political implications. During the war, they should set such an example by demonstrating toward the various governments-in-exile a degree of cordiality which corresponds to the strength of democratic and anti-fascist tendencies which each manifests. It is for the Soviet government then to make its own choice.

So much for the Anglo-American security sphere in Western Europe which is no problem and the Soviet security sphere in Eastern Europe which is a problem but not one to the solution of which Britain and America can make a great direct contribution.

Germany, however, belongs neither in one sphere nor in the other. As long as Germany remains patently bellicose and aggressive, what to do with Germany causes no discord among the super-powers. With German military power smashed, her industrial machine in ruins, and her fascist rulers toppled from the seats of power, decisions as to the future regime of Germany cannot be delayed. The structure of three-power collaboration could hardly survive a failure to agree on the urgent problems raised by a defeated Germany. Since the pressures brought to bear upon Germany from the East and from the West will be of something like the same magnitude, the United States, Britain, and the Soviet Union will of necessity have to take each other's desires into account. Can their common agreement upon the necessity for anti-fascist regimes in Europe provide the basis for collaboration?

The Roosevelt-Churchill formula of "unconditional surrender" postponed public announcement, and perhaps also official agreement, respecting Germany's future. The Atlantic Charter (Point 3), however, seems to have promised "all peoples" the right to live under a form of government of their own choosing. This right presumably will be granted to the German people, although it will not include the right again to choose a fascist form of government.* Will this right be exercised through free elections with universal suffrage conducted under United Nations supervision? Or will it be implemented by delivering the government over to a politically advanced group not unfriendly to the United Nations cause and who might be expected to know what the German people would have wanted or ought to have wanted if their natural democratic impulses had not been thwarted by a decade of Hitlerite tyranny? Will there be an inter-Allied supervisory authority during the transition to the new democratic Germany, or a division of German territory between the principal occupying powers, or a United Nations-sponsored regime, or some combination? If some or all internal government is to be put in German hands prior to any free election, should this government be constituted on broad nonparty lines or should it have a definite party complexion?

One hopeful sign of agreement on problems of this type is the convergence of key symbols in the political vocabulary of leaders of the three super-powers. The Teheran Declaration speaks of a "world family of democratic nations." The parliamentary democracies of the West have in recent times been

---

* Winston Churchill has repeatedly warned the world that the Atlantic Charter does not constitute "a bargain struck" with Germany, and that Germany after surrender could make no claims under it. It is, however, a bargain struck with elements of British and American public opinion to which a new German government might appeal.

refurbishing their somewhat austere democratic dogma with symbols calculated to give men assurance against the insecurities of modern urban life. "Full employment," "social security," "national planning" are now commonplaces even in conservative speech. Soviet leaders have meanwhile sought to incorporate the most potent symbols from the West. They stress the rights of smaller nations to cultural autonomy within the Soviet Union and political autonomy without. They expose "tyranny and slavery, oppression and intolerance." To counter the National Socialist conception of a "New Order," a hierarchy with Nazi Germany at the apex, they offer a formal equality of nations, with national liberation for all "freedom-loving peoples." The use of vocabularies which in part overlap does not, however, eliminate the possibility of disagreement, for a variety of meanings may be read into these symbols.

The Declaration Regarding Italy,[8] which resulted from the Moscow Conference of October, 1943, gave concrete formulation to the often stated common anti-fascist aims. There is a promise "that the Italian people shall be given every opportunity to establish governmental and other institutions based upon democratic principles." There is agreement that the new government must include elements which have always opposed fascism. Civil rights are to be restored in full measure and to include freedom "to form anti-Fascist political groups." A beginning in the restoration of democracy is to be made by creating "democratic organs of local government," but presumably there will be for a time tutelage at the national level. Finally, there is agreement that paramount military considerations may delay giving full effect to these principles, with the proviso that any one of the three governments may invoke a discussion of the application of this provision.

Italy is more nearly in the Anglo-American security sphere than in the Russian, as the strategy pursued in the present war clearly indicates. Nevertheless, it is the first *ex*-enemy power. The pattern followed in developing an anti-fascist successor government is of intense interest. It is in a way fortunate that the Italian experience in evolving a regime acceptable to all three super-powers is available at the time when the vastly more crucial decisions respecting Germany must be made. Delays and miscalculations in implementing the Declaration Regarding Italy have not been fatal to the future of three-power collaboration, for the continuing German threat has held them riveted together. When the final collapse of Germany is achieved, however, there will not be time for prolonged negotiation between Moscow, London, and Washington. With the lessons learned from Italian experience there need be neither delay nor failure in agreeing upon the necessary, immediate steps to be taken.

Meanwhile, the Manifesto of the Moscow-sponsored National Committee of Free Germany [9] offers some further clues as to the type of Germany which Moscow envisions. The Committee refers to itself as "people with the most different political views and convictions, who only a year ago would have considered such unification impossible." If the new German government, like the Committee, is to enjoy the support of persons with widely divergent political views, German patriotism rather than class or party allegiance must be the criterion of selection. This suggests either a government of nonpolitical personalities or a broad nonparty government uniting anti-fascist elements of both left and right. The good faith of the new government in pursuing an anti-fascist course would be tested, according to the Manifesto, by (1) its "annulment of all laws based on national and racial hatred," (2) "the immediate release of the victims of Hitlerite terror and material compensation for the damage caused them," (3) "the restoration and extension of the political rights and social gains of the working people," and (4) its establishment of "the guaranteed right to labor and to lawfully acquired property." Some of these tests would be more appropriate if the allegedly nonparty regime were to have in fact a liberal-democratic orientation. The leftist-liberal character of the regime would be further assured if Moscow's proposals for the reduction of the power of the Junker class through the cession of East Prussia to Poland should be adopted.

The first and second items are in harmony with the program adopted for Italy, and the third and fourth could only be the product of long-term policy. They probably represent the minimum social program for a regime which is to make sucessfully the transition to an enduring postwar democratic government. Announcement of such a program, therefore, need not be a subject for discord between the powers at the time of the cessation of hostilities.

Even if the goal agreed upon is the kind of Germany for which moderately progressive elements worked during the Weimar regime, this does not mean that a particular party is to be charged with the responsibility for postwar government. Liquidating the war will have many unpleasant aspects, and having to act under the close supervision of a foreign authority would doom any party government to the stigma of being the agents of foreigners.

It would be inappropriate to expect or to permit the German people to choose prematurely the particular anti-fascist constitutional system under which they are to live. Until the political practices upon which free elections depend, viz., free speech, free assembly, free press, and free association, have begun to function effectively again, elections would be meaningless. Certainly, Allied supervision ought to be sufficient to guarantee that a spontaneous expression of public opinion takes place at the time of the choosing of the first true party government. The scope of inter-Allied intervention in German domestic affairs would be lessened in proportion as the stability of its democratic institutions was demonstrated. This, however, raises again the question of super-power agreement on basic objectives, for decisions as to the maintenance or withdrawal of inter-Allied supervisory agencies will require that Britain,

America, and the Soviet Union continue to agree on the minimum requirements of "anti-fascist democracy" which the German government must show.

If the Soviet Union were to insist upon a communist Germany, there would be no such agreement, but for many reasons it seems clear that there will be no requirement from Soviet Russia that the postwar German political system parallel that of the Soviet Union in every respect. One is that a sovietized Berlin might tend to replace Moscow as the ideological and political capital of the communist world. Another is that Soviet Russia does not seem to be prepared to fight a third world war to achieve this end and could hardly achieve it otherwise.

There is a third reason why a truly democratic Germany would correspond to the practical state interests of the Soviet Union, as well as to those of the Western-democratic superpowers. The rigidity of a regimented, undemocratic German social system would inhibit the nice adjustments which alone could make German policy satisfactory to all the super-powers. In their quest for a stable political equilibrium in Europe, the three powers must strive not only to make cheap and profitable aggression impossible—this, we have already said, requires opposition to the consolidation of Europe under the hegemony of any power—but also to make unlikely revolutions and coups d'état which freeze in power totalitarian and inflexible regimes. Each super-power will wish to see Europe so organized that the possibility of its becoming a fourth super-power or of its being used in offensive action by another existing super-power is minimized.

Toward Germany and other countries which do not clearly lie within the zones of paramount interest of any one of the super-powers, the interests of the Big Three in promoting democratic tendencies may well coincide.* A power bloc in the

---

* They have a reciprocal interest in promoting decentralizing and democratic tendencies in each other's home countries. The American position toward Russia would be much improved *if* the monolithic structure of Russian so-

German or any other "neutral" area so great in extent or so tight in organization as to make possible a sudden disadvantageous shift in the power position of one of the super-powers is, from their point of view, mutually undesirable. Here, then, is the realists' reason for preaching and working for an extension of democratic values under the banner of the "four freedoms." This conclusion need not shock those who regard the extension of democratic values as a good in itself, for it is surely no argument against the promotion of democratic tendencies everywhere in the world that it improves the security position of the United States.

Once the victorious United Nations armies have been repatriated, each government will find it difficult to move its army beyond the confines of its own territory. The Moscow Declaration further enjoins them by its sixth provision "not [to] employ their military forces within the territories of other states except for the purposes envisaged in this declaration and after joint consultation." The peace-time pressure which they could bring upon Germany unilaterally is therefore limited. It is not, however, sufficiently limited to prevent serious conflict between the Western powers and the Soviet Union if there is basic disagreement as to the regime to be promoted within Germany.

The role of the United States as the chief exporter of goods will no doubt be matched by a Soviet role as the chief exporter of inflammatory symbols. Whether the American goods are sent to Germany as a gift, a bribe, a loan, or as payment for goods received from Germany, the American capacity to affect the functioning of Germany's postwar political system will be great. These inflowing goods may, for example, be used to

ciety were modified to permit appeal to groups within Russia which might moderate official policy in the direction desired by the United States. Possibilities in this direction, it must be confessed, are slight. The Soviet position in bargaining with the United States is obviously stronger for being able to appeal to politically influential or politically discontented groups within the United States to bring pressure to bear upon their government.

strengthen the middle-class groups with the most pronounced Western prodemocratic tendencies. They may, on the other hand, be used to rebuild German heavy industry and to reestablish the political dominance of its former owners with tendencies both anti-democratic and anti-communist. To reconstitute some of the formerly powerful groups in Germany and in the rest of Europe might create regimes which for internal reasons would seek to deflect the discontent of the masses by stirring up the "Red" bogey. If American goods are used to guarantee certain minimum standards of nutrition in Germany after the collapse, the choice of the channels of the distribution will be politically significant. On the assumption that the Soviet Union is more likely to choose pacific means to attain security if it does not feel threatened from the West, the United States has every reason not to permit the flow of goods or investment into Germany to be unnecessarily provocative to the Soviet Union.

A similar moderation on the part of the Soviet government in controlling the flow of revolutionary propaganda into Germany and Western Europe is also desirable. It will in fact be shown if there is a continuing agreement among the three peripheral powers as to the kind of Germany which they wish to encourage. The dissolution of the Communist International and the willingness of Communists everywhere in the world to merge their activities into movements organized on the basis of a broad patriotic nonparty appeal are no guarantees of future moderation. They do indicate a line of policy which, if pursued, would make Anglo-American-Soviet collaboration throughout the period of German reconstruction more feasible.

The victorious United Nations need not prescribe in detail the institutions of an anti-fascist German democracy. It is enough if they agree on the minimum requirements which these institutions must meet and agree for the rest to permit Germany freely to develop her own institutions. To prescribe in detail would be to impose democracy, a contradiction in terms; it might also help to promote an anti-democratic reaction. If any one of the super-powers were to set requirements in addition to the program to which all have agreed, conflicting counter-requirements from the other super-powers would destroy the basis of three-power collaboration.

On the bases of (1) opposition to consolidation of Europe under the hegemony of Germany or any other power, (2) recognition of each other's special security interests in areas nearest their own borders, and (3) agreement on the minimum requirements for anti-fascist democracy in Germany and Europe generally, collaboration among the super-powers appears feasible. Beyond this, they must agree collectively to "nonintervene." From the point of view of the super-powers themselves such nonintervention would assure them of a European buffer zone which would give them security from each other.[10] From the point of view of Europe, it would give that continent scope for the autonomous development to which its high civilization entitles it.

VIII. The Economy of Joint Action

> *It would be a master stroke if those great Powers honestly bent on peace would form a League of Peace, not only to keep the peace among themselves, but to prevent, by force if necessary, its being broken by others.*
> THEODORE ROOSEVELT, in a speech accepting the Nobel Peace Prize, 1910.

TRIPARTITE collaboration in Europe is *feasible* on the twin bases of "no regimentation either of persons or of peoples." Is is also an *efficient* method for advancing the interests of each super-power?

Until a sense of world citizenship becomes more widespread than it is at present, the burden of proof will be on those who advocate collaboration to demonstrate that that alternative is the more efficient way for one's own country to achieve maximum security. If it is also more efficient for the rest of the world and for one's partners in collaboration, that is so much to the good; but it is not the decisive consideration.

Each of the major powers will of course seek to protect its interests by unilateral as well as by collective action. Whether a given power will emphasize the "lone-hand" or the "collective" aspects of its policy depends upon which course of action is judged to be the most efficient in terms of its own national interest. Perfect security without any commitment to protect any other power is perhaps theoretically the "ideal" solution.

Certainly if a state could dwell in complete safety without joining coalitions or international organizations which might take it into war to defend another power against aggression, it would be unlikely to abandon an isolationist course. Similarly, if a modest or ambiguous commitment were to bring as great security as an extensive and precise one, most states would choose the former.

In its period of "splendid isolation" Britain was able to rule the ocean world because the political organization of Europe kept that continent "in balance" without Britain's having to add its weight to either side to prevent the overturn of the balance. Thus, in the period of the Pax Britannica, security from European aggression was achieved without commitment. The Soviet Union, in its temporarily successful effort to turn the present war to the West, also won a measure of security through isolation. The oft-expressed distaste of the United States for joining in "Europe's wars" reflects a belief that this country can achieve a greater measure of security in isolation than in collaboration with other powers.

According to traditional balance-of-power thinking, each of the super-powers ought to prefer a situation in which the two other super-powers compete for its favor. A number of considerations, however, point to collaboration as the efficient course for each to attain its own national objectives. Those already discussed include: the comparative invulnerability of the Anglo-American bloc and of the Soviet Union from attack by the other; the extreme improbability of resort to war as a mode of settling Anglo-American disputes; the approximate territorial satiety of all three; and the greater risk from Germany than from each other. To these may now be added the principle of the economy of joint action.*

---

* The Moscow Declaration in its preamble based the need for tripartite collaboration upon the principle of economy of joint action when it recognized "the necessity of insuring a rapid and orderly transition from war to peace and of establishing and maintaining international peace and security

A coalition policy for achieving security would be backed by the combined military potential of the three super-powers and their smaller allies. This pooled strength would be even greater than is sometimes supposed, for it is more than the algebraic sum of the potentials of the powers taken separately. The technological, raw material, and geographic assets of each, supplement deficiencies of the others. The strategic interdependence of the United States and Britain has already been discussed. In the present war, as Max Werner has written:

> The potentialities of the Red Army are necessarily restricted by the Soviet Union's industrial resources. The Red Army cannot have more arms available than can be produced out of twelve to fifteen million tons of steel. The Red Army cannot outrun the *Wehrmacht* in its mass of offensive weapons. The military power of the Anglo-Saxon block, on the other hand, is limited by its circumscribed land power. But combined, the Anglo-American-Soviet coalition is ahead of the Third Reich in economic as well as in military might.[1]

From the geographic point of view also they reinforce each other:

> Germany has a safe hinterland in Western Europe only in fighting against the Soviet Union, a safe hinterland in Eastern Europe only in fighting against the Anglo-American block. But against the combined anti-Hitler coalition she has no safe hinterland whatever.[2]

Sir Halford Mackinder, in his usual metaphorical style, has also described the advantages of a coalition peace strategy.

> . . . the polluted channel [Germany] might be swept clear very effectively if it were controlled by strong embankments of power on either hand—land power to the east, in the Heartland, and sea power to the west, in the North Atlantic basin. Face the German mind with an enduring certainty that any war fought by Germany must be a war on two *unshakable* fronts, and the Germans themselves will solve the problem.

with the least diversion of the world's human and economic resources for armaments."

For this to happen it will be necessary in the first place that there be effective and lasting coöperation between America, Britain and France, the first for depth of defense, the second as the moated forward stronghold—a Malta on a grander scale—and the third as the defensible bridgehead. The last is no less essential than the other two, because sea power must in the final resort be amphibious if it is to balance land power. In the second place, it is necessary that those three and the fourth conqueror, Russia, be pledged together to coöperate immediately if any breach of the peace is threatened, so that the devil in Germany can never again get its head up and must die by inanition.[3]

For the Soviet Union a coalition security policy has a special advantage. The ribbon of steel which binds the Soviet West and the Soviet Far East, the Trans-Siberian Railroad, is so thin that the government will want to insure itself against simultaneous trouble at the two ends of the line. Only a Japan which was fighting for its life in China and the Pacific and fighting against the mounting Anglo-American strength would have refrained so long from invading Vladivostok and the Soviet Union's Far Eastern provinces.

Tripartite collaboration is both feasible and efficient. It would eliminate in advance doubt as to the outcome of a new challenge from Europe or East Asia. There is, however, a further prerequisite to its acceptance as the cornerstone in the structure of the postwar international order. That is an expectation on the part of each of the super-powers that neither of the other two will revert in a crisis to a policy of isolationism. It does not follow that a coalition security program which ought on rational grounds to appeal to each of the Big Three will necessarily seem attractive to each partner in the prospective coalition. Not only must it be in the American interest, but Americans must believe that it is more in the American interest than any other alternative now suggested. Russians must believe that it profits the Soviet Union. Great Britain and the Dominions must view it as the most effective scheme available for maintaining what they consider to be their vital interests.

Britain and Russia, by their twenty-year defensive alliance, have already registered their agreement that the security of each as well as the general security of Europe must rest on joint effort. How to make even more certain that Soviet leaders will wish to collaborate has already been discussed at length. What assurance can the United States give of its continued responsible participation in supporting the new peace? Many believe that without a modification of the Senate's role in foreign affairs there can be no assurance against a reversion to isolationism.[4] If such a modification is to be effected through the processes of formal constitutional reform, this is a counsel of despair since the prospects are slight for constitutional amendment in time to influence the coming peace. Public opinion may permit the by-passing of the Senate in the making of peace, but it may not.[5] Americans must therefore grant that the possibility of American isolationism is not negligible. They must expect their chief partners in enforcing the peace to examine with care the risks to which this prospective isolationism exposes them.

The elements of the new American isolationism are already well-known.[6] By asking "Where will Stalin stop?" and "Why doesn't Russia fight Japan?" the new isolationist line creates doubt as to whether Stalin's successes are not really defeats for our way of life and even as to whether we have not entered the war on the wrong side. The isolationists' emphasis on "Japan First" may appeal to our third great ally, China. When, however, the justification given is the necessity for exterminating "those yellow monkeys," a poor basis is laid for long-run Sino-American friendship. Our partners in peace have, then, some need to be reassured. The resolution introduced by Senator Connally and passed November 5, 1943, by an overwhelming 85-5 majority of the Senate substantially incorporated into its text the formulae of the Moscow Declaration. It is from the point of view of our present allies a favorable omen, but it has not served to quiet all their fears.

Downing Street and the Kremlin have long memories. They will wonder whether the chorus of approval for postwar international collaboration is a product of a change of heart or of a passing mood. Even the war-time chief executive has passed through isolationist phases. Subscribing wholeheartedly to the "munitions-maker devil theory of war" with all its isolationist connotations, President Roosevelt declared in his Chatauqua address of August 14, 1936:

. . . if war should break out again in another continent, let us not blink the fact we would find in this country thousands of Americans who, seeking immediate riches—fools' gold—would attempt to break down or evade our neutrality. . . . To resist the clamor of that greed, if war should come, would require the unswerving support of all Americans who love peace.

If we face the choice of profits or peace, the Nation will answer— must answer—"We choose peace." . . .

At this late date, with the wisdom which is so easy after the event and so difficult before the event, we find it possible to trace the tragic series of small decisions which led Europe into the Great War in 1914 and eventually engulfed us and many other Nations.

We can keep out of war if those who watch and decide have a sufficiently detailed understanding of international affairs to make certain that the small decisions of each day do not lead to war, and if, at the same time, they possess the courage to say "no" to those who selfishly or unwisely would let us go to war.[7]

Diplomats of other countries will also remember the purely verbal character of American opposition to international lawlessness in the 1930's. This is epitomized in an official report of Secretary Hull's conversation of July 6, 1937, with the Italian ambassador, Fulvio Suvich. The Secretary said that the United States *"while taking every precaution to keep aloof from political and military involvements abroad,* strongly feels that each civilized country right now has the unshirkable responsibility of making a real contribution to promote peace."[8] Even after the fall of France the Secretary declared in a conversation of June 28, 1940, with the British ambassador and the Australian minister "that everything possible was being done '*short of a serious risk of actual military hostilities*' to keep the Japanese situation stabilized."* This conversation was followed within three weeks by the Anglo-Japanese agreement of July 14, 1940, to close the Burma Road for a period of three months.

Will the United States again wait until its first line of defense in Europe and its second line in the Western Pacific have been breached before it begins to experience acute feelings of insecurity? Its prospective partners in peace would like to know the answer. In retrospect many Americans now wish that the United States had done more, sooner, in order that it might not have had to do so much, later.† Will they and their successors be able to apply the moral of retrospective analysis to the prevention of prospective crises?

Victorious democracies, especially if they have been spared the ravages of war in their own homelands and especially if they have been drawn into war reluctantly, are likely to find the fruits of victory bitter. Forgetting that the fruits of defeat would have been incomparably more bitter, they may in retro-

---

* *Peace and War*, Washington, Government Printing Office, 1943, p. 94. Italics mine. This quotation and the previous one are not introduced as indictments of Secretary Hull's policy but as demonstrations of the unwillingness of competent United States authorities to make any commitments whatever which might ultimately have to be backed with force.

† Walter Millis, for example, in a passage striking for its candor, writes of his own previous isolationism, as follows: "It might seem as though I were describing a campaign conducted in a vacuum. It might seem so; and unfortunately that, I believe, is exactly what it was." "The Faith of an American" in *America in a World at War*, Series No. 3, New York, Farrar and Rinehart, 1941, p. 20.

Charles and Mary Beard in their *The American Spirit*, p. 615, gently chide their former companions in isolationism for their too complete adaptation to the exigencies of the Second World War. They write that "after the war broke out in Europe in 1939, critical thinking about civilization in the United States became unfashionable in many quarters."

spect come to view the war as somebody's else quarrel into which they unselfishly but quixotically plunged. This time it will not be England which will feel this way, for the Battle of Britain has permanently destroyed any notion that the continent is far away. In America, however, Europe may possibly again come to seem a remote area which our ancestors left for very good reasons. Unilateral disarmament by the United States may again be widely favored because it will seem to promise compulsory nonparticipation in the next holocaust.* Such disarmament would of course guarantee nonparticipation at the time when aggression could be most easily checked, before it occurs. It would guarantee that the United States would have actively to participate only at the eleventh hour. Our participation, when it came, would in that case have to be total. The United States would be involved in a third and even bloodier struggle, whose outcome, moreover, would be doubtful.

When Franklin D. Roosevelt promised "to keep war out of America," he meant presumably that any fighting by Americans would be done along lines of defense far removed from the boundaries of America's continental homeland and that the economic, diplomatic, and ultimately if necessary the military policies of his administration would be to support whichever powers were defending these lines. American future policy ought accordingly to be oriented toward the minimum objective of keeping war out of America and the maximum objective of keeping war out of the world.

The lethargy which besets victorious democracies in peace time is disastrous, but the danger of it is real and the danger of American lethargy is as real for America's chief allies as for the United States itself. A variety of public opinion polls have

* To the extent that a "peace movement" is successful only in the United States and such other countries as have no thought of expansionist aggression, it turns the balance of power in favor of the would-be aggressor and thus by its success constitutes an invitation to aggression. Cf. Quincy Wright, *A Study of War*, Chicago, University of Chicago Press, 1942, Vol. II, pp. 1350-51.

testified to the war-time willingness of most Americans to see the United States participate in some form of postwar international collaboration.* This was also true in 1920 when the voters chose between party platforms which advocated, in the case of the Democratic party, participation in *the* League of Nations and, in the case of the Republican party, participation in *a* League of Nations. They chose the latter and got participation in *no* League of Nations. After the Second World War they may be more insistent and persistent, but the mere fact that during war they favor collaboration is no clear evidence of their postwar preferences.

Our chief collaborators in any proposals for enforcing security will nevertheless want to know the least that can be expected from the United States. What is the irreducible minimum of American participation in enforcing the new peace? Is that minimum sufficient to guarantee victory in the event of a new challenge to general security? Great Britain and France have not in the past found the speculative possibility that the United States might, in case of war, but only after two or three years, come to their aid, a sufficient foundation upon which to build a collective security policy. Their leaders have sometimes indicated that the potential impact of the United States is so enormous that it is essential to have a reasonably clear understanding of what the United States will or will not do.

In predicting the course of American foreign policy our prospective collaborators should bear in mind the following considerations:

(1) Membership in the League of Nations did not in every case guarantee wholehearted collaboration in collective security policies; and American nonparticipation did not mean complete irresponsibility in the matter of checking aggression. It is by no

* See National Opinion Research Center, *The Public Looks at World Organization*, Report No. 19, April, 1944, showing that in every section of the country more than seventy per cent of those interviewed favor active participation by the United States in postwar world politics.

means clear that American membership in the League of Nations would have insured the success of League measures to check aggression at the time of the Manchurian and Ethiopian incidents. Success or failure in securing United States adhesion to a multilateral instrument to promote peace may be less important as evidence of future American policy than an analysis of past behavior.

(2) If there is any single thread running through American policy toward intervention in Europe's politics, it is "no prior commitments." The United States has never been willing to tell Europe or the world what it would do in case of a war which might or might not occur. It has not been willing to tell because it did not yet know. Its inclinations were so clearly toward "staying out" that it has always chosen to remain aloof as long as there was hope that nonparticipation would be possible. "No prior commitments" has not, however, always been followed by nonparticipation.

(3) American behavior in two world wars gives some clue as to America's probable behavior in the event of a third world war, if that catastrophe should take place. Twice the United States has intervened to prevent the overturn of the balance of power in Europe by the Caesar who was then challenging it.*
With or without prior agreement the United States will take a hand when its people recognize the necessity for so doing. They have twice recognized this necessity before any aggressor became invincible. If potential aggressors and potential victims of

---

* In no period of general war in Europe since the inception of the republic has the United States been able to remain at peace. Cf. Quincy Wright, *An American Foreign Policy Toward International Stability*, Chicago, University of Chicago Press, 1934, pp. 1-8. Professor Wright has also shown in his *A Study of War*, Vol. I, Appendix XIX, pp. 625-35, how rare it is for any great power to remain at peace in a period of general war. Participation, however, was in many cases strictly limited. Only in the twentieth century has a system of general wars been inaugurated which, if the war is prolonged, seems almost inevitably to guarantee the full-scale participation of all powers of the first rank.

aggression both remember this, challenges to the new world order may not be so lightly made.

(4) America's inescapable interest in Britain's security has already been discussed in detail. It is a further guarantee that in any world crisis United States weight will ultimately be thrown into the balance in opposition to the aggressors.

Great Britain, the Soviet Union, and the other partners in checking Hitlerite aggression cannot therefore legitimately reason that American irresponsibility and spasmodic isolationism make a peace program based on super-power collaboration impractical. Their governments may with cause complain if the United States should again be unwilling to make specific commitments to implement its continuing denunciations of "international lawlessness"; but this should not blind them to the constructive role which the United States would play, even though unwillingly, in any program of great-power collaboration to check aggression.

The irreducible minimum of American participation is enough to guarantee a better fate for Britain and the Soviet Union than would be theirs if either of them reverted to isolationism. For the United States, immediate and continuing collaboration in peace with her war-time allies offers so much greater dividends than spasmodic, reluctant, compulsory, and eleventh-hour participation that there is a very good chance that Britain and the Soviet Union can have full American collaboration. In the least favorable case, a new aggressor would be defeated. In the most favorable case, he would be discouraged from making the challenge which would have to be put down by war.

IX. The Super-Powers and the World Community

God help Israel, if the prophets ever get the upper hand!
　　　　Abiathar in "Giant Killer" by Elmer Davis

SUPER-POWER collaboration as a program for maintaining peace in the postwar world has so far been examined chiefly from the point of view of the super-powers themselves. This has been done on the assumption that the major threats to peace in the postwar world will come from conflicts among these powers. According to one group, however, even though it may be necessary for the Big Three to have the dominant influence in the postwar security system, "There is real danger that they will use their power largely in their own interest with a corresponding disregard of the rights or claims of the smaller powers. . . . the influence of the great powers can be decreased by including all the smaller powers in the international organization, and by requiring a majority vote of all members on important matters of policy. The small powers are by nature peace-loving and opposed to aggrandizement through aggression, and will serve as an admirable check on the few great powers."[1]

Whether there is in fact a great-power interest which is in opposition to the interest of small powers is open to question. The United States and Great Britain are not more aggressive than Thailand or Poland. Within those federal systems in which there are several "great" states, such a conflict has not developed. Prussia, as the only great member-state in the German federal system, may have developed a set of interests opposed to those of the other German states. History has not, however, demonstrated that New York, Pennsylvania, Illinois, and Texas have, as large states, interests which conflict with those which New Hampshire, Rhode Island, Delaware, and Nevada have as small states.

The great powers have a common interest in preventing cheap and successful aggression by a power such as Nazi Germany which aspires to hegemony over all of them. There is no other security interest which they share with each other.* This one common interest they share with the small powers.

It is not joint enforcement of security by the collaborating super-powers which the smaller nations have to fear. Their moment of danger would come if the great powers fell apart. With the failure of tripartite collaboration each of the super-powers would seek to enhance its own power position by reverting to an isolationist emphasis on the consolidation of its own security sphere. In that event many of the smaller states would have to place their sole reliance for security on the good will of a single great neighbor. Curiously enough, Richard Olney, whose influence was so great in demarcating the whole New World as the United States' special security sphere, has stated most concisely the small-power interest in collective great-power action:

> When great states agree among themselves as to the international relations of other and weaker states, they at the same time also put restraints upon themselves. They virtually check the ambition and

---

* If all the great powers were to develop expansionist policies simultaneously, there might be a limited period of "peace" at the expense of the small powers which lay within their respective orbits of domination. Since, however, Britain and the United States are nonexpansionist, there is virtually no possibility of a partition of the rest of the world among the three super-powers.

aggressiveness of all parties to the agreement and thus furnish a guaranty of the propriety and sincerity of their purposes impossible to be furnished by a single state in the same position.[2]

As a nineteenth-century German international lawyer, rationalizing the principles upon which the Concert of Europe was based, has written:

> It is natural that the smaller states should be less able to resist the collective political action of the great powers. But their voluntary submission to the unanimous counsel of the great powers, through which there is attained at least a strong presumption of the existence of a collective international interest, is more beneficial to their juridical position than that submissiveness to the threats of individual neighboring states of superior power which formerly prevailed.[3]

Many of the leaders of the present governments-in-exile have explicitly recognized that the *sine qua non* of small-state security is great-power collaboration. C. J. Hambro, former President of the Norwegian Parliament, has declared:

> It is the demand of all the small nations that the leaders of the great countries shall be strengthened and not thwarted in their efforts. . . .
>
> More and more clearly the small nations recognize that any attempt to disseminate distrust among those great nations, that any appeal to national prejudice, to old jealousies and fears between the big countries, is a menace to every small State.[4]

Dr. Eduard Beneš, leader of the Czechoslovak government-in-exile, in a widely publicized address of February 2, 1944, was more explicit, declaring: "Munich and all the European disasters that followed could have come about only because of Western Europe's hostility to the Soviet."[5] Dr. Beneš explained how the Czechoslovak government was turning to the East, to Moscow, for its primary guarantee of security, how this guarantee had been given in the Soviet-Czech treaty of alliance of December, 1943, and how this alliance was underpinned by the Anglo-Soviet treaty of May, 1942. The latter agreement provided the legal basis for continuing collaboration between the great powers to the East and to the West. It therefore was insurance against a repetition of the type of disaster which befell Czechoslovakia at Munich.

To say that peace in Europe and in the world during the next generation depends in the first instance upon the active collaboration of the super-powers, sometimes leads to the charge that one is favoring an "undemocratic" organization of the postwar world. It is said to be undemocratic because it arrogates decisive influence in the decisions which determine questions of war and peace to the three great states in a world in which there are twenty times that number of sovereign units. Here, too, the realistic leader of Norway may be quoted:

> Every small nation will have to give up the cherished idea that her influence in world affairs should be just as great as that of any other nation. . . .
>
> In any universal organization, no matter what name be given to it, a few great countries will have to bear the burden of carrying out the ultimate decisions of the world authority, and to those countries must be given, constitutionally, the formal power corresponding to their real and factual responsibility.[6]

It is not necessary to accept Dr. Hambro's proposal to recognize the great powers' role by giving them a special constitutional status, but one should note his emphasis on "their real and factual responsibility." Is he thereby dissenting from the principles of "sovereign equality" as a basis for a general international organization in the postwar world? Does his recognition of the special role of the greatest powers imply an acceptance of an undemocratic world organization? To answer this question some consideration should be given to the extent to which precepts derived from a study of a democratic society of individuals should properly be applied by analogy to a world society of independent states.

States, like individuals, should have an equal right to protection in a system of law. It is as hateful that a small state's right of existence be jeopardized just because it is small as it is that a poor person be victimized because he lacks the money to hire a clever lawyer. A classic statement of this sentiment is that of Elihu Root at the Second Pan-American Scientific Congress, December 30, 1915. He declared:

> We believe in the independence and the dignity of nations, and while we are great, we estimate our greatness as one of the least of our possessions, and we hold the smallest state, be it upon an island of the Caribbean or anywhere in Central or South America, as our equal in dignity, in the right to respect and in the right to the treatment of an equal.[7]

The analogy between states and individuals should not, however, be carried too far. States, like individuals, have unequal influence in the realm of politics. Individuals in the liberal-democratic societies of Western European origin have, if judged to be "fit," equal suffrage as of right. Even where suffrage is denied, the individual is almost always potentially a voter—as soon as he becomes adult, or becomes naturalized, or establishes continuous residence for a certain period in the community. "One head, one vote" implies a rough equality in the right to formal participation in policy-making. The broader the electorate, the more democratic the society is thought to be.

Human beings are potentially equal in a sense that states are not, and progress toward equalizing the benefits of modern technology and toward equalizing the influences of all individuals in the political process is considered progress toward a democratic society. The poor are potentially rich. Siam is not even potentially a Soviet Union, nor is Honduras potentially a Britain.

International government designed to equalize the influence of states would not necessarily make for a more democratic organization of world society. The toll which the silver Senators have levied on the United States Treasury as the price of political co-operation with the Democratic party is an example which should discourage one from advocating a legislative assembly in the postwar world organization in which representation is equal for large states and small. New Yorkers and New Mexicans may have accommodated themselves to this particular abuse, but Russians and Paraguayans will not.

The difficulties of complete adherence to the principle of equality of participation in the international political process were most clearly illustrated in the Second Hague Peace Conference of 1907. Westlake illustrated the spurious character of the "equality" which was adhered to in voting by citing the fate of a British proposal to abolish contraband of war. The vote was twenty-six states in favor of the proposition with four —France, Germany, Russia, and the United States—opposed. When Great Britain attempted to unite the twenty-six in a treaty to give effect to their votes, all but Haiti refused. He concluded that "on . . . democratic principles, there was bound to come the equality of votes for the purpose of display, and with that . . . the worthlessness of votes for any purpose but that of display." [8]

A London *Times* editorial referred to the "excessive prolongation of the labors of the conference . . . mainly due to . . . the obstinacy of the South American states." [9] The European small states had an interest in having a coherent great-power leadership because their very existence depended upon it. On the other hand, the small states far removed from the major zone of power conflict permitted their theoretical interest in equality to determine their behavior. It does not make international organization more "democratic" to make it as easy for Uruguay as for the United States to obstruct effective action.

The alternative to equality, a carefully calculated inequality, is also impracticable as a method of achieving the values of democracy at the international level. Were size of population the basis for computing representation, China and India would receive voting quotas wholly unacceptable to most of the other states. If wealth, reputation for power, reputation for not being aggressive, capacity to assume international responsibility, or some combination of these were used as indices, the prestige factors involved would be so troublesome that the task of allocating voting would have to be abandoned long before it was completed.

If formal equality and carefully calculated inequality of state representation in the real decision-making body of the new general international organization are both unsatisfactory, what is left? The Covenant of the League of Nations sought to escape this dilemma by concentrating effective power in a Council which included as permanent members all of the Great Powers and as temporary members a rotating representation of the smaller powers.

On paper, the League of Nations seemed to have power adequate to restrain an aggressor. What were the fatal defects which reduced it to complete impotence in the crisis of general war? A Soviet commentator, B. Shatrov, has concisely summarized them as follows: (1) the absence from the Council table for fourteen years of a representative of the Soviet Union and for twenty years of one from the United States, (2) the "pseudo-democratic" requirement of unanimity which permitted veto by an uninterested small power or by a small power which was acting as the agent of an aggressor power to sabotage sanctions, (3) the conception of the League as an entity independent of its members, which permitted "an evasion of responsibility for political decisions by various governments (chiefly the prewar governments of Great Britain and France)," and (4) the exclusion of the cardinal security problems from Council jurisdiction because the Great Powers chose to settle them through other agencies.[10] The Conference of Ambassadors in Paris, the Washington Conference of 1921-22, the naval conferences at Geneva in 1927 and at London in 1930, and the discussions leading to the Nonintervention Agreement with respect to the Spanish Civil War, all dealt with problems which properly were within the purview of a central organization for the maintenance of security.

If voluntary co-operation of the anti-fascist great powers had been achieved, action through the League Council would have been unnecessary. Without such co-operation it was irrelevant.

Too great emphasis in contemporary discussion on the mechanical or structural aspects of international co-operation to preserve the peace obscures the really vital problem, how to develop among the super-powers a disposition to consult and to agree.* The present effective co-ordination of policy as between the independent members of the British Commonwealth of Nations demonstrates that a spirit of collaboration is even more essential than a machinery. There are in fact no formal organs for determining policy binding on the whole Commonwealth. The strides toward tripartite collaboration made at the Moscow and Teheran conferences suggest further that face-to-face contact between the principals accomplishes a co-ordination of which no League Council manned by subordinates would be capable.

It might perhaps be better if the powers of the first rank developed strictly *inter se,* and therefore outside the general international organization, the procedures for arriving at joint decisions. There could be no valid objection to any arrangement by the Big Three by which they promised each other to act together to preserve general security and, thereby, security for each. With that assured, three troublesome problems would be avoided. In the first place, voluntary co-operation would obviate the need for formal labeling of "first-rank" and "lesser" states in the covenant of the general postwar international or-

---

* Secretary Hull recognized the voluntary aspect of international action to prevent successful aggression when he declared: "A system of organized international cooperation for the maintenance of peace must be based upon the *willingness* of the cooperating nations to use force, if necessary, to keep the peace." "Bases of the Foreign Policy of the United States," March 21, 1944, text in New York *Times,* March 22, 1944. Italics mine.

ganization. In the second place, fears about "sacrificing sovereignty," which are generated by debates over a nation's entry into a universal organization, would not have the same opportunity to paralyze the will to collaborate. As Carl Becker has written, "Let us not, then, irritate national egoism or offend the pride of sovereignty by inaugurating the union with flourish of trumpets, impressive ceremonies, and pledges given and taken for all future time." [11] Finally, collaboration outside the general organization would eliminate the danger that effective great-power collaboration could be prevented by the opposition of isolated small states who were either satellites of the power against whom action was to be taken or whose stake in the particular decision reached and whose responsibility for enforcing it were of a lesser order.

Formal commitments made by one super-power to come to the aid of another must be backed by a continuing will to collaborate. The dismemberment of Czechoslovakia in 1938 at Munich brought about the complete destruction of the Soviet Union's diplomatic defenses, built as they were around the Franco-Soviet defensive alliance of 1935. The Munich Conference thus demonstrated to the world that it was not in formal commitments but in a will to friendly collaboration among all the great powers opposed to aggression, i.e., between the Western democratic powers and the Soviet Union, that the key to general security could have been found.

This does not mean that commitments are of no importance. An adamant unwillingness to be committed is interpreted as a determination not to engage in friendly collaboration. Sir Norman Angell has reported that he acted as an intermediary for M. Herriot in proposing that Ramsay MacDonald's government give France a guarantee against attack by Germany in case France had offered and Germany had refused to arbitrate the dispute which preceded the attack. Herriot was further willing that England should give a similar guarantee to Germany to come to Germany's aid in case France should, after refusing an offer of arbitration, attack Germany. MacDonald is reported to have replied that "if France behaves well there is virtually no chance that the Boche will attack." In effect, he said, according to Sir Norman: "The end of all these undertakings to go to war if this, that, or the other thing happens, is that we *shall* go to war." [12] Such an attitude on the part of any of the leaders of the great states would of course put an end to the effectiveness of any organization for peace based on preponderant power, whether it proposed to act through informal collaboration or through a more formalized machinery of international organization.

Almost equally encouraging to a prospective aggressor are diplomatic declarations which are highly general in denouncing aggression and highly specific in promising not to implement the declaration in any way. An illustration is Norman Davis' statement, with the express authorization of President Roosevelt, to the Geneva Disarmament Conference on May 29, 1934:

> We are prepared to cooperate in every practicable way in efforts to secure a general disarmament agreement. . . . We are furthermore willing . . . to negotiate a universal pact of nonaggression and to join with other nations in conferring on international problems. . . . *The United States* will not, however, participate in European political negotiations and settlements and *will not make any commitment whatever to use its armed forces for the settlement of any dispute anywhere.*[13]

Secretary Hull's New York speech of February 16, 1935, established as the "four pillars of peace": (1) *renunciation* of war as an instrument of national policy, (2) *promise* of nonaggression, (3) *consultation* in the event of a threat to peace, (4) *noninterference* on our part with measures of constraint brought against a deliberate violator of the peace.[14] Although this may have been the most constructive contribution which American public opinion would permit him to make toward dissipating the storm clouds of aggression,* the first three "pillars" are promises only of verbal action and the fourth is a promise *not* to do something in the event of crisis. It seemed therefore to preclude any broad organization of the "peace-loving" great powers into a combination which would intimidate Hitlerite Germany in advance of an actual crisis, and which would give French and British statesmen the courage to oppose firmly Hitler's first challenges to the Versailles order. It has been argued elsewhere † that the *ultimate* alignment of the United States with a coalition to put down great aggressors may be confidently predicted. What the world needs after this war, however, is not still more United Nations military victories over the Hitlers of successive generations but more occasions when such men are stopped before titanic conflict has broken out. This requires American participation before the eleventh hour and the fifty-ninth minute.

If it were true that in any given decade the probable aggressor's identity was a mere matter of conjecture, agreements to take action against "the aggressor" such as were embodied in Articles 10-16 of the old League Covenant would constitute the sole valid type of commitment. One could then echo Woodrow Wilson's praise of that Covenant for accomplishing the "disentanglement of all alliances" when he said that by it "Nations promise not to have alliances. Nations promise not to make combinations against each other. Nations agree there shall be but one combination, and that is the combination of all against the wrongdoer." ‡

* This speech did commit the Department of State not to interfere with the operation of League sanctions under Article 16 by pressing its neutral rights, in case it agreed with the League's identification of the aggressor.

† Cf. *supra*, pp. 137-39.

‡ New York address, March 4, 1919, text in Saul K. Padover, ed., *Wilson's Ideals*, Washington, American Council on Public Affairs, 1943, p. 120. Cf. Secretary Hull's statement in "Bases of the Foreign Policy of the United States," *loc. cit.*: "As the provisions of the four-nation declaration are carried into effect, there will no longer be need for spheres of influence, for

In fact, the number of possible major disturbers of the peace is limited to the six or eight states with the greatest war potential. The United States and the British Commonwealth are definitely not expansionist-minded. China's great difficulty is to develop military efficiency adequate to consolidate her present territories. France, also, as a power of declining relative war potential in a continent of declining relative war potential, is on the defensive. The very great danger of setting up the Soviet Union as the target of anti-aggression agreements has been discussed *in extenso*. Germany and Japan thus remain as the only major powers whose tendency to aggression would have to be checked by special arrangements. Military action to check their expansion should not be delayed by the operation of cumbersome machinery to "identify the aggressor."

Specific arrangements designed to operate in the contingency of a new German or Japanese challenge do not violate the Wilsonian conception of no combination except "the combination of all against the wrongdoer." Contingent commitments would operate only against these powers if they again put themselves beyond the pale. By being ready in advance, however, they would decrease the probability of a new attempt at carving out *Lebensraum*.

With continuing consultation and agreement among the three greatest powers, guarantees could be given the less powerful neighbors of Germany and Japan. In the League, Germany's smaller neighbors backed collective action until it became clear that League guarantees were unreliable and that the leadership of the peace-minded great powers had failed. In a program for peace depending upon the informal collaboration of the superpowers these smaller neighbors might be expected to participate

alliances, for balance of power, or any other of the special arrangements through which, in the unhappy past, the nations strove to safeguard their security or to promote their interests." Presumably, *until* the provisions of the four-nation declaration are carried into effect, there will be need for some "special arrangements."

voluntarily to the extent that their own interests were directly involved. It is most important, of course, if the super-powers wish to retain their good will and spontaneous co-operation that no decisions affecting any of the smaller states be taken except after representatives of the affected states have been consulted.[15] Even in the early days of the European Concert of Powers this was recognized when the leaders of the five great powers at Aix-la-Chapelle agreed that "in the event of such reunions [meetings of the Sovereigns or of their representatives] having for their object the condition of other states in Europe, they shall not take place except in pursuance of a formal invitation to those by whom these states are directed, and under an express reservation of their right to participate directly or by their repesentatives." [16]

Note the analogous undertaking in the Moscow Declaration for the Big Three to consult with each other and "as occasion requires," with themselves defining the occasion, with other powers. The Big Three because of their great inherent power, the mobility of that power, and their correlated far-flung interests and responsibilities will be automatically concerned with any threat to the peace and must especially regard as a menace *any* attempt by the defeated members of the Axis coalition to embark on a new career of conquest. Other powers not immediately threatened would not be asked to take immediate action.* On this basis also one provides for the important position of such great regional powers as France and China. Later perhaps, when they develop a leadership that can win the confidence of world opinion in their peaceful intentions, Germany and Japan would be in the same category. Prime Minister Churchill's proposal for a Council of Europe and a Council of

* This corresponds to the distinction at the Paris Peace Conference between "powers of general interest" and "powers of special interest." For a discussion of the Dominions in the British Commonwealth as "powers of special interest," see H. W. V. Temperley, ed., *A History of the Peace Conference of Paris*, London, Frowde, 1924, Vol. VI, pp. 342-60.

Asia would permit these regional great powers to function where their own interests were involved. The more remote smaller powers would less frequently be expected to assume responsibilities. The inner decision-making core in any given crisis would thus vary according to the issues involved. It would include the regional great powers more or less as a matter of right in consultations affecting the security of their own regions.

What relation would the general security organization envisaged by the Moscow Declaration have to the tripartite assumption of major responsibility for enforcing peace? It is well to be precise regarding its function because so much of the present public discussion of "a League with teeth" is led by men who say: "Either you create a true international police force—or else!" The "or else!" constitutes a prediction that otherwise the Third World War is certain to follow in no distant future. Since there cannot be such an international police force created at this stage in world history, such an admonition diminishes the real chance that a contribution can be made to peace on the basis of the voluntary co-operation of the greatest powers. It will prematurely and unnecessarily discourage those whose support is most necessary if a reversion to isolationism is to be avoided.

The world nevertheless needs a general security organization if only to symbolize the real world-wide community of interest in checking aggression. The act of creating the international organization would have high educative value in accustoming peoples to the conception of their common stake in security. By having the formal plenary sessions of this organization held at various capitals throughout the world, the full ceremonial possibilities of the organization as an educational device could be exploited. In this respect the practice of the Pan-American Union might well be emulated.

Furthermore, with such an organization functioning it would be possible for the informal procedures based on collaboration around a three-power nucleus to be carried on explicitly in the name of the organized world community. This would not only reaffirm the universal interest in checking aggression, it would provide a supra-national justification for assumption of special responsibilities by the great powers which the smaller states could accept with no sense of derogation of status and which the peoples of the great powers could accept with no sense of resort to illegitimate dominance or hegemony. This universal organization could be used to validate whatever direct action the super-powers take which could not await the operation of the organization's necessarily cumbersome machinery. Such a validation would make it clear that the super-powers were not acting exclusively in their own interests. If a challenge to the world order involved prolonged hostilities which had not been put down by the time the organization acts, such a validation would facilitate small-power acquiescence in measures which narrowed their rights as neutrals but hastened the restoration of order.

There is another advantage in referring to a world organization a case which might involve policing action by one or more of the super-powers. The League of Nations' successes in the 1920's in settling disputes between small powers illustrate this advantage. By acting through a supra-national organization, the Great Powers brought a halt to violence without that stoppage being construed as an improvement in the position of one of the first-rank powers at the expense of the others. Thus, the existence of an institution which furnishes a unifying symbol for all states increases the chance that the actions of the leading powers will be construed as nationally "anonymous" and on behalf of a greater whole.

Were a true international police force to be set up, there would no longer be "super-powers," "regional great powers," and "small powers." Threats to the peace anywhere would evoke action by the supra-national agency. However, until such

---

* In Chapter I this contingency was judged to be remote.

a police force begins to function,* there will continue to be gradations of power and responsibility among states. Effective collaboration to check aggression must be built on the distribution of power in the world we will have to live in. In this world a self-constituted coalition of first-rank powers must be the nucleus of a general security program.

X. Coalition for Peace: a Program for Our Own Time

There is a wide choice of instruments once a morale exists.
  WALTER LIPPMANN, in "The Stakes of Diplomacy"

THERE are a variety of frameworks of commitments within which a three-power coalition for peace could operate. The elements of one such framework, which are suggested by the present volume, may for convenience be brought together at this point. They consist of the following: (1) a unilateral declaration by the United States of its determination to uphold a strong, friendly, independent, and democratic Britain and a reciprocal declaration by Great Britain of a determination to support the American position in the Western Pacific; (2) a multilateral agreement signed by the Big Three, the other United Nations, and such other "freedom-loving" states as desire to sign, which sets up a noncoercive general security organization for "a world family of democratic nations"; (3) an exchange of identical notes directing the Combined Chiefs of Staff (British and American), in the light of the two unilateral American and British declarations and the multilateral undertakings, to engage in joint planning after the war ends for effective and immediate action to check aggression; * (4) the

---

* The same intimate co-ordination of action and interpenetration of each other's planning activities which is achieved by the Anglo-American Combined

Anglo-Soviet treaty of defensive alliance which establishes the indivisibility of Europe as a security problem; (5) a three-power declaration regarding Europe and especially Germany, stating the twin objectives of anti-fascist democracy and anti-"New Order" independence for the peoples of Europe; (6) treaties of defensive alliance between some of Germany's smaller neighbors and the adjacent super-powers; (7) a three-power declaration guaranteeing the administrative and territorial integrity of China and engaging the three powers not to supply factions within China with the instruments of war to use against each other; * (8) a three-power undertaking to consult at the request of any one of them regarding the implementation of any of these agreements to which all three are parties.

Super-power collaboration is not offered as a complete program for insuring either world peace or universal justice. In at least three respects it is deficient. (1) It does not deal with the problem of peaceful change. (2) It makes no provision for the growth of "welfare" activities at the supra-national level. (3) It is not in itself a program for permanent peace.

If by "the problem of peaceful change" one means discovering an equitable procedure for persuading a power to accept without war changes which formerly could be accomplished only by war, including even modifications of its frontiers, then the problem has not been solved. There may be cases in which rectifications of boundaries can be accomplished voluntarily or

---

Chiefs of Staff need not be extended to include the Russian and Chinese military planning authorities. In the typical case of checking aggression, an exclusive three-power force would not be called into play. Only in case of a global threat to world order would the forces of all three move. Even then they might, as in the Second World War, fight separate but parallel campaigns.

* See the forthcoming volume by David N. Rowe, cited *supra*, p. 18. While the consolidation of Western Europe would be a major threat to the super-powers, the *fragmentation* of China might bring them into conflict with each other.

under informal pressure, but there is small prospect that now or in the future peaceful procedures will develop which give nations what they have hitherto thought it worth fighting to get.[1] Instead, one should seek to give *men* things so that they will not collectively seek as nations that which they will be denied and which they will then fight for. As David Mitrany has written, "The only sound sense of peaceful change is to do internationally what it does nationally: to make changes of frontiers unnecessary by making frontiers meaningless through the continuous development of common activities and interests across them."[2] The problem of peaceful change, when seen as the problem of lessening geographical restrictions on individual activities, would be largely solved by making provision for the growth at the supra-national level of "welfare" activities.

This is not the place to solve that problem. It is sufficient only to point out that a series of political agreements which will provide future generations with physical security provides also the essential atmosphere within which agreements on such matters as the revival of a world trading system or the regulation of world shipping or international labor legislation become possible. Whether "welfare" activities at the supra-national level ought to be carried on under the aegis of the general security organization promised in the Moscow Declaration has been argued pro and con.[3] But whatever the conclusion in this regard, the complete irrelevance of armed power as an index of a state's influence in solving international welfare problems should be emphasized.*

---

* Even acting separately and in terms exclusively of its own national interest, the great state has sometimes found that it cannot afford to squander its power in day-to-day frictions with small neighbors. If it seeks to force solutions to trade and other essentially nonsecurity questions by threatening to use its overwhelming force, it only denies itself the possibility of evoking the spontaneous co-operation of its small neighbors in a war crisis. Cf. Jacob Viner, "International Finance and Balance of Power Diplomacy, 1880-1914," *Southwestern Political and Social Science Quarterly*, March, 1929, pp. 407-

The super-powers may or may not in the case of a given function be the powers with the greatest legitimate interests. In the regulation of merchant shipping, for example, Britain and America have a great stake. The Soviet Union has a lesser one. Norway, in this particular field, has a stake out of all proportion to her military might. For the super-powers to insist that as super-powers they are *ipso facto* entitled to leadership in every international conclave and to a *liberum veto* in every international conference would blight the future growth of much needed international institutions. It would also threaten the stability of the peace which rests on three-power collaboration, for leaders of lesser powers could say with some plausibility that only by becoming themselves first-rank powers could their own free development be assured.

The legitimacy of the final criticism, that super-power collaboration is not a complete program for permanent peace, may be freely conceded.* It is a peace program for our own time. It is not a grand design for a brave new world in which the menace of war has forever disappeared. Grand designs are important. They furnish analytical models for public discussion of important problems. They provide criteria by which to test the long-run consequences of various short-run alternatives. Most grand designs are, however, presented by their authors as the one best hope of avoiding a fresh descent into the maelstrom of global war.

The Germans, in the 1920's and 1930's, wanted the world

51; idem, "Political Aspects of International Finance," *Journal of Business*, April, 1928, pp. 141-73, and July, 1928, pp. 324-63. W. B. Harvey, *Tariffs and International Relations in Europe, 1860-1914*, Private Edition, University of Chicago Libraries, 1938, has demonstrated that "no case can be made out for any significant correlation between political and tariff friction." The lack of correspondence between power alignments and extent of economic co-operation suggests that the small powers were not generally coerced when the stake was primarily economic.

* Cf. Mortimer Adler, *op. cit.*, for a discussion of the problems involved in such a complete program.

to believe that it was the sin of Versailles, the failure of the leaders of 1919 to choose the one right plan for reconstruction of the world, that was driving them to a fresh trial by battle. They wanted the world to forget that many of Germany's troubles after 1918 flowed not from the peace but from the war itself. The impoverishment of the middle classes and the psychological difficulties caused by defeat may be mentioned. Many of the rest of Germany's and the world's troubles flowed not from the peace treaties but from mistakes made during the twenty-year "long armistice." The world is not going to be saved forever, no matter how skillfully the coming peace treaties are drawn up; nor is it going to be lost forever, no matter how badly the job is done. The best of treaties will still leave difficult problems to solve; the worst will not be so bad that it cannot be made worse by bungling in the postwar period.

It is therefore not a legitimate argument against a program of super-power collaboration that it fails to guarantee permanent peace. To the criticism that it seems to offer no sure solution to the dimly foreseen problems of 1970 or 2070, one can make two comments. (1) History is a succession of transition periods whose problems need to be solved one period at a time. (2) A program of effective three-power collaboration will at least not reproduce in 1970 the 1939 situation in which a solution without world war seemed unavoidable.

The statesmen of any given decade have an obligation both to their own time and to the future. They have an obligation to their own time not to purchase "permanent" peace by fighting to win a war which, by the obsolescence or peaceful settlement of the dispute which engendered hostilities, might have proven unnecessary. The chance that all three of the super-powers will in the foreseeable future voluntarily turn over their arms to the control of a supra-national authority is infinitesimally small. To fight to disarm one or more of them in order to create a world-state would violate the obligation not to engage in unnecessary war which today's statesmen have to our own time.

To the future their obligation is to choose that path toward peace which makes recourse to general war in another generation as little likely as possible. Super-power collaboration provides a method for eliminating lesser disputes while they are still "lesser."

As for the "major" disputes, conflict between the super-powers is not impossible. Were any one of the super-powers to develop an appetite for unlimited expansion, the other super-powers would organize the world, including the immediately threatened small powers, against it. To meet this catastrophic contingency statesmen must prepare a "second-line" policy. For Britain and America this would be to constitute themselves into a nucleus around which much of the rest of the world—except the new seeker after world hegemony—would gather. A preponderant organization of power in favor of stability and peace having been destroyed, because of a defection by one of the super-powers, the others would have to move to redress the threatened balance. The frequently maligned balance-of-power principle thus would operate to insure that the preponderant strength of the greatest powers when used jointly is used only to promote general security, i.e., "freedom from fear." Balance is the sanctioning mechanism which makes peace via preponderance practical. Balance of power is therefore not banished but rather sublimated into socially constructive channels.

Super-power collaboration has the negative virtue of being a program which would not repeat the error of the early 1920's. The opportunities of total victory were after the First World War so inadequately exploited by the Franco-British-American coalition that won the war that in fifteen years no trace of their joint leadership remained. After this war a Soviet-Anglo-American collaboration can maintain the peace at least until the basic pattern of world politics has been redefined and that coalition has become obsolete.

A generation of continuous collaboration might destroy any hope of political success for German public figures who would seek to drive a wedge between Soviet Russia and the Western democracies. It might thus pave the way for the readmittance of Germany into the postwar order with a degree of influence which would correspond to its inherent war potential. With the growth of "welfare" activities at the international level might come the broader universal moral consensus which would permit new steps toward a still more lasting peace.

A Soviet-Anglo-American coalition for prolonging peace is not sufficient to guarantee permanent peace. It does offer real promise that the next twenty years will be a transition to something other than a third world war.

NOTES

Notes

CHAPTER I (pp. 3-11)

1. See Lionel Gelber, *Peace by Power*, New York, Oxford University Press, 1942, who stresses the wholly beneficent role which Anglo-American armed might can play in the present age.
2. Cf. H. Foster Anderson, *Borderline Russia*, London, Cresset, 1942, p. 193, for an anecdote in which this metaphor is used to expose another logical fallacy.
3. *The Federalist*, No. XI. In this same essay Hamilton foreshadows the Monroe Doctrine when he observes that "our situation invites and our interests prompt us to aim at an ascendant in the system of American affairs." In general on the skill of the Founding Fathers in balance-of-power analysis and on their conclusion that United States security depended on European interests in the New World being kept in balance, see Edward Mead Earle, "National Security and Foreign Policy," *Yale Review*, Spring, 1940, pp. 444-60, and "Political and Military Strategy for the United States," *Proceedings of the Academy of Political Science*, January, 1941, pp. 112-19; also, Alfred Vagts, "The United States and the Balance of Power," *Journal of Politics*, November, 1941, pp. 401-49.
4. *U. S. Foreign Policy: Shield of the Republic*, New York, Little, Brown, 1943, p. 29.
5. In a letter to Lieutenant Commander W. W. Kimball, November 19, 1897, Roosevelt advocated war with Spain and thereby "taking one more step toward the complete freeing of America from European domination." Quoted in H. F. Pringle, *Theodore Roosevelt*, New York, Harcourt, Brace, 1931, p. 176. "McKinley, who hoped for peace, had," according to Pringle, "brought to Washington a young man who, within the decade, had been favorably inclined toward war with Mexico, Chile, Great Britain, Spain, and all European powers so arrogant as to hold colonies in the western half of the world." *Ibid.*, p. 171. It is to be noted that the most flamboyant of his letters were written in the 1890's. As President he well understood the necessity for a responsible executive to match his words to fit the existing power situation.
6. Henry Adams, *Education of Henry Adams*, Boston, Houghton Mifflin, 1918, pp. 421-25.
7. On the "sporting" attitude prevalent in America toward "big shots" who are "lucky" enough to get rich, see H. D. Lasswell, *World Politics and*

Personal Insecurity, New York, McGraw-Hill, 1935, p. 218. This same attitude may carry over into power politics, where a big navy like a big bank account may be viewed as a scoring device to record "success."

8. Cf. Sumner Welles, *The World of the Four Freedoms*, New York, Columbia University Press, 1943, pp. 34, 61.

9. For peace to depend upon the more or less accidental coincidence of objectives of the policies of the great states is objectionable to many. Walter Lippmann is attacked in the *New Yorker*, February 19, 1944, pp. 15-16, for advocating a policy based on the self-interest of the United States. The *New Yorker* urges instead that American policy be "to bring an end to the use of policy" by working to create "constitutional world law" and "government on a planetary level."

10. Cf. Edward Mead Earle, "American Military Policy and National Security," *Political Science Quarterly*, March, 1938, p. 5.

CHAPTER II (pp. 12-24)

1. See Bernard Brodie, *Sea Power in the Machine Age*, Princeton, Princeton University Press, 1941, pp. 160-67, for a discussion of Britain's differential advantage in an age of transition from wooden to iron hulls.

2. See Harold and Margaret Sprout, *Toward a New Order of Sea Power*, Princeton, Princeton University Press, 1940, Chapters I and II, upon whose analysis of the rise and decline of British maritime supremacy the present discussion is based.

3. U. S. Department of State, *Papers Relating to the Foreign Relations of the United States, 1895*, Vol. I, Washington, Government Printing Office, 1896, p. 558.

4. Sprout, *op. cit.*, pp. 279-80.

5. Friedrich List was the first to appreciate "the influence of railways upon the shifting balance of military power." Edward Mead Earle discusses List's remarkable insights in his essay, "Adam Smith, Alexander Hamilton, Friedrich List: The Economic Foundations of Military Power," in *Makers of Modern Strategy*, Princeton, Princeton University Press, 1943, pp. 148-52.

6. For a brief essay in an almost totally neglected field of research in military history, see T. H. Thomas, "Armies and the Railway Revolution," in *War as a Social Institution*, J. D. Clarkson and T. C. Cochran, editors, New York, Columbia University Press, 1941, pp. 88-94.

7. "Memorandum on the Present State of British Relations with France and Germany," Foreign Office, January 1, 1907, in G. P. Gooch and Harold Temperley, editors, *British Documents on the Origins of the War, 1898-1914*, London, His Majesty's Stationery Office, 1928, Vol. III, p. 404.

8. See Thomas, *loc. cit.*

9. Cf. Arnold Wolfers, *Britain and France between Two Wars*, New York, Harcourt, Brace, 1940, pp. 3-4.

CHAPTER III (pp. 27-49)

1. On the major categories of historic controversy, see C. R. Fish, "The United States and Great Britain, 1776-1930," in *The United States and Great Britain*, Chicago, University of Chicago Press, 1932, pp. 1-78.
2. The text of the Polignac memorandum is found in the *British and Foreign State Papers*, 1823, Vol. XI, pp. 49-53.
3. *Loc. cit.*, p. 419. This interpretation of the British position in the 1820's differs substantially from that of Walter Lippmann. In his *U. S. Foreign Policy: Shield of the Republic*, pp. 16-22, he interprets the Monroe Doctrine as evidence of a tacit Anglo-American alliance. Professional historians who have criticized Lippmann's position on the Monroe Doctrine include: S. F. Bemis, "Walter Lippmann on U. S. Foreign Policy," *Hispanic-American Historical Review*, November, 1943, pp. 664-67; A. P. Whitaker, "Our Pan American Policy and the Post-War World," *Harvard Educational Review*, October, 1943, pp. 285-300; and C. C. Tansill, "Mr. Lippmann on American Foreign Policy," *Thought*, September, 1943, pp. 403-10. This comment is by no means a criticism of Lippmann's conclusion regarding the *present* identity of British and American foreign-policy objectives.

On the diplomatic background of the Monroe Doctrine in Anglo-American relations, see S. F. Bemis, *The Latin American Policy of the United States*, New York, Harcourt, Brace, 1943, Chapters IV and V.

4. Cf. Lionel Gelber, *The Rise of Anglo-American Friendship: A Study in World Politics, 1898-1906*, New York, Oxford University Press, 1938. Alfred Vagts has made the interesting suggestion that "the history of these Anglo-American relations is best understood when it is conceived of not so much in the terms of the Rise of Anglo-American Friendship, but rather in those of the Reduction of Anglo-American Hostility." *Loc. cit.*, p. 418.

5. There were many who forecast such a war. Cf. Sir Norman Angell, "An Englishman's Point of View," in *The United States and Great Britain*, pp. 87-94. Those who believed that trade rivalries breed war were most certain that armed conflict could not be avoided. Friedrich List, who had earlier advocated a continental alliance to check British power, was in the 1840's warning Britain to make an alliance with Germany and the other continental powers while there was yet time in order to protect herself against the young titan across the Atlantic. List, *The National System of Political Economy*, New York, Longmans, Green, 1904, pp. 339-40, cited by Earle, "Adam Smith, Alexander Hamilton, Friedrich List: The Economic Foundations of Military Power," in *Makers of Modern Strategy*, p. 147.

6. Speech of July 13, 1928. Text in his *Leninism*, London, Modern Books, 1933, Vol. II, p. 124.

7. Cf. Gelber, *The Rise of Anglo-American Friendship*, pp. 80, 102, for evidence of John Hay's exasperation at his inability, for reasons of domestic politics, to accept proffered British co-operation at the time of the Boxer Rebellion and to secure, on the part of the United States Senate, a more

gracious acceptance of British concessions regarding Isthmian Canal policy, which were embodied in the Hay-Pauncefote treaties.

8. Cf. U. S. Senate, Special Committee on the Investigation of the Munitions Industry pursuant to S. Res. 206, 73rd Congress, *Munitions Industry*, Washington, Government Printing Office, 1935-36, 7 vols. The reference is to the Nye committee hearings.

9. New York, Simon and Schuster, 1937 and 1939. On the dupe or scandal theory of American involvement in the First World War, there are many books not all of which are specifically anti-British but whose total effect was to inhibit American support of any program to check fascist aggression. Cf. C. Hartley Grattan, *Why We Fought*, New York, Vanguard Press, 1929; Walter Millis, *Road to War*, Boston, Houghton Mifflin, 1935; Frederick Palmer, *Our Gallant Madness*, Garden City, Doubleday, Doran, 1937.

10. Reading the text and supporting documents of *Peace and War*, Washington, Government Printing Office, 1943, the Department of State's own apology for the ineffective course of American diplomacy in the decade 1931-41, one is struck by the purely verbal character of American foreign policy. It is difficult for Americans now, as it must have been for the British then, to understand the necessities of the domestic political situation which reduced America's role in the developing crisis to the reiteration of sterile generalizations.

11. *The American Senate and World Peace*, New York, Vanguard Press, 1944, p. 115. See also R. J. Dangerfield, *In Defense of the Senate*, Norman, University of Oklahoma Press, 1933, for a careful survey of the occasions on which the Senate has refused its consent, or given it only conditionally, or postponed action so long as to defeat the purpose of the executive. He concludes that the Senate makes its influence felt less by failing to approve treaties than by casting doubt in advance as to whether it will approve treaties and thus materially altering the treaties brought forth for its approval.

12. Cf. Sigmund Neumann, *Permanent Revolution*, New York, Harper, 1942, for a discussion of the origin of modern dictatorship in terms of these three groups.

13. Hiram Motherwell, *The Peace We Fight For*, New York, Harper, 1943, stresses the primacy of the food problem in postwar planning.

CHAPTER IV (pp. 50-69)

1. *The Atlantic System*, New York, Reynal and Hitchcock, 1941, p. 249.

2. On the eve of the Second World War an "Islands for War Debts Committee" was organized whose program, as the name indicates, included a proposal for the United States to take over the British West Indies in return for cancellation of part or all of the inter-Allied debt of the First World War. Its real purpose was to prolong the period of American neutrality, and

the committee proved to be a transmission belt for Nazi propaganda. J. R. Carlson, *Under Cover*, Philadelphia, Blakiston, 1943, pp. 128-29.

3. New York *Herald Tribune*, December 22, 1943.

4. Vagts, *loc. cit.*, p. 436.

5. Cf. Sprout, *op. cit.*, pp. 260-67. Cf. also "Arms Limitation Agreement Gives Britain Control of Atlantic," *Army and Navy Journal*, December 17, 1921, p. 371; and Captain Dudley W. Knox, "Four-Power Treaty Gives Advantage to Great Britain and Japan," *ibid.*, December 31, 1921, p. 413.

6. Pp. xii-xiii.

7. On the outbreak of the Second World War, M. J. Savage, then Prime Minister of New Zealand, declared: "Both with gratitude for the past and with confidence for the future we range ourselves without fear beside Britain—where she goes we go—where she stands we stand. We are only a small young nation but we march forward with a union of hearts and wills to a common destiny."

8. Cf. N. J. Spykman, *America's Strategy in World Politics*, New York, Harcourt, Brace, 1942, and *The Geography of the Peace*, New York, Harcourt, Brace, 1944.

9. This fact is recognized by the highly literate, even if widely diffused and therefore politically ineffective, elements in the American population which almost instinctively have begun to buy books on Anglo-American relations in a time of mutual danger. In the Second World War, as in the First, authors and publishers have been quick to meet the demand. Some volumes stress the "common heritage" aspect of Anglo-American relations, e.g.: R. B. Mowat and Preston Slosson, *History of the English-Speaking Peoples*, New York, Oxford University Press, 1943; Philip Gibbs, ed., *Bridging the Atlantic*, New York, Doubleday, Doran, 1944. Several propose federation or some other special constitutional tie between the United States and the British Commonwealth of Nations, e.g.: George Catlin, *Anglo-Saxony and its Tradition*, New York, Macmillan, 1939; Clarence Streit, *Union Now with Britain*, New York, Harper, 1941; Lord Davies, *Foundations of Victory*, London, Collins, 1941, and *Facing the Future*, London, Staples and Staples, 1942. Still others stress strategic interdependence, e.g.: John MacCormac, *Pax Britamericana*, London, Routledge, 1943, and books already cited by Forrest Davis and Lionel Gelber.

10. For these and similar quotations, see Forrest Davis, *op. cit.*, pp. 60, 106, 116-17, 130-31.

11. *Peace by Power*, pp. 126-27.

12. Cf. Angell, *loc. cit.*, pp. 118-21.

13. London, Gollancz, 1940.

14. *The Public Papers and Addresses of Franklin D. Roosevelt*, New York, Macmillan, 1941, 1938 volume, p. 493.

CHAPTER V (pp. 73-91)

1. *Op. cit.*, pp. 436-40.
2. A London *Times* editorial of February 29, 1944, favors the creation anew of a "strong" Germany, presumably favorable to British interests.
3. Sir Eyre Crowe noted in 1907 that a policy of continuous concession and of liquidating all outstanding sources of difficulty had in twenty years not fundamentally improved Anglo-German relations. *Loc. cit.*, p. 407. One practical consequence of the calculation to be made respecting Soviet foreign policy is that it will determine how far attempts should be made to conciliate the Soviet government. Those who believe that too many concessions are being made will criticize their government for appeasing Stalin.
4. See D. J. Dallin, *Russia and Postwar Europe*, New Haven, Yale University Press, 1943.
5. *Democratic Ideals and Reality*, New York, Henry Holt, 1919, 1942.
6. On Russian-American diplomatic relations in general, see Foster R. Dulles, *The Road to Teheran*, Princeton, Princeton University Press, 1944.
7. "We Must Face the Facts About Russia," *Reader's Digest*, July, 1943, p. 12.
8. *Congressional Record*, May 17, 1943, pp. 4574 and 4576.
9. Stalin used this phrase in replying to a question submitted to him by Ralph Parker, New York *Times* correspondent, May 4, 1943.
10. *The Russian Enigma*, New York, Scribners, 1943.
11. *Op. cit.*
12. Cf. Maurice Dobb, *Soviet Economy and the War*, New York, International Publishers, 1943, Chapter VI, and A. Yugow, *Russia's Economic Front for War and Peace*, New York, Harper, 1942, Chapter VII.
13. For text of this Manifesto, see New York *Times*, August 1, 1943.
14. See Joachim Joesten, *What Russia Wants*, New York, Duell, Sloan and Pearce, 1944, pp. 89-92, for a translation of extensive passages from this declaration.
15. See Frank W. Notestein and others, *The Future Population of Europe and the Soviet Union*, Geneva, League of Nations, 1944.
16. *Ibid.*, p. 56.
17. *Ibid.*, p. 134.
18. New York *Herald Tribune*, April 4, 1944.

CHAPTER VI (pp. 92-106)

1. *Battle for the World*, New York, Modern Age, 1941, p. 117.
2. See Robert Strausz-Hupé, *Geopolitics*, New York, Putnam, 1942, Chapter XV, for an exposition of Lord Curzon's conception of a "belt of frontiers." This is a related conception but on a continental scale.
3. On the American interest in preventing the consolidation of the rim-

land areas, see N. J. Spykman, *The Geography of the Peace*, New York, Harcourt, Brace, 1944.

4. Notestein and others, *op. cit.*, p. 264.

5. Dallin, *op. cit.*, Chapter II, argues that Lenin and Stalin have always preferred collaboration with Germany to collaboration with the Western democracies and, *ibid.*, pp. 208-19, that the Soviet Union may envision a strong Germany after the present war.

CHAPTER VII (pp. 109-28)

1. Arnold Wolfers, "In Defense of the Small Countries," *Yale Review*, Winter, 1944, pp. 201-20, defends the small power against the charge that it is an anachronism which contributes to the military and economic instability of Europe. For a pessimistic estimate of the future viability of small powers in Europe, see E. H. Carr's discussion of "the crisis of self-determination" in his *Conditions of Peace*, New York, Macmillan, 1942, Chapter III.

2. The replies of twenty-six European governments to Briand's "Memorandum on the Organization of a Régime of European Federal Union," of May 17, 1930, were almost without exception equivocal and unenthusiastic. For the texts of the Briand proposal and the twenty-six replies, see *International Conciliation*, June, 1930, Special Bulletin, and December, 1930.

3. *Contra*, see many recent books advocating European federation which seem to have had a wider appeal in Britain and America than in continental Europe, e.g.: Alfred M. Bingham, *The United States of Europe*, New York, Duell, Sloan and Pearce, 1940; Lord Davies, *A Federated Europe*, London, Gollancz, 1940; W. Ivor Jennings, *A Federation for Western Europe*, New York, Macmillan, 1940; Abraham Weinfeld, *Towards a United States of Europe*, Washington, American Council on Public Affairs, 1942; Richard N. Coudenhove-Kalergi, *Crusade for Pan-Europe*, New York, Putnam, 1943.

4. Frans Van Cauwelaert, "Dangers of a European Federation," *Belgium* (New York), April 2, 1942, p. 48. It is from this same article that the quotation which opens Chapter VII is taken.

5. Cf. Margaret Mead, *And Keep Your Powder Dry*, New York, William Morrow, 1942, pp. 234-50.

6. Cf. Czech-Soviet Treaty of Mutual Assistance, December 12, 1943.

7. See Joesten, *op. cit.*, pp. 89-92. Cf. "The Polish Question," *Information Bulletin*, Embassy of the U.S.S.R., Washington, March 16, 1944, a translation of an article in *War and the Working Class*, for similar evidence.

8. Text in New York *Times*, November 2, 1943.

9. Text in New York *Times*, August 1, 1943.

10. Cf. Arnold Wolfers, "Anglo-American Post-war Coöperation and the Interests of Europe," *American Political Science Review*, August, 1942, pp. 656-66, and especially p. 663, for the conception of Europe as a "cushion or buffer zone."

CHAPTER VIII (pp. 129-39)

1. Max Werner, *Attack Can Win in '43*, Boston, Little, Brown, pp. 164-65.
2. *Ibid.*, p. 165.
3. "The Round World and the Winning of the Peace," *Foreign Affairs*, July, 1943, pp. 601-02.
4. Cf. Colegrove, *op. cit.*, Chapter VIII.
5. The American Institute of Public Opinion's release of October 13, 1943, indicates that a great majority of the American people are unaware of the present method of treaty approval and would prefer approval by a majority of both houses of Congress. The reaction might have been different if those interviewed had first been told the present constitutional provisions.
6. Selden Menefee, in his *Assignment: U. S. A.*, New York, Reynal and Hitchcock, 1943, Chapter XIV, has described them.
7. *The Public Papers and Addresses of Franklin D. Roosevelt*, New York, Random House, 1938, Vol. V, pp. 290-92. Quincy Howe, in his *Blood Is Cheaper Than Water*, uses substantially this same quotation as a keynote quotation for his whole volume.
8. *Peace and War*, pp. 367-68. Italics mine.

CHAPTER IX (pp. 140-55)

1. Universities Committee on Post-war International Problems, "Should There Be An International Organization for General Security Against Military Aggression, And Should the United States Participate in Such An Organization? Summary of replies received from the Cooperating Groups on Problem IV," mimeographed [1944].
2. Richard Olney, "The Development of International Law," *American Journal of International Law*, April, 1907, p. 425.
3. Franz Holtzendorff, *Handbuch des Völkerrechts*, Berlin, 1885-89, Vol. II, p. 16, quoted and translated in Edwin D. Dickinson, *The Equality of States in International Law*, Cambridge, Massachusetts, Harvard University Press, 1920, p. 139.
4. Speech of January 22, 1944, New York *Times*, January 23, 1944.
5. New York *Times*, February 4, 1944.
6. *Loc. cit.*
7. Reprinted from Elihu Root, *Latin America and the United States*, Cambridge, Massachusetts, Harvard University Press, 1917, p. 292.
8. J. Westlake, "The Hague Conference," *Quarterly Review*, January, 1908, p. 229, quoted in F. C. Hicks, "The Equality of States and the Hague Conferences," *American Journal of International Law*, July, 1908, p. 546.
9. October 21, 1907, quoted in Hicks, *op. cit.*, p. 539.
10. B. Shatrov, "The League of Nations," *Information Bulletin*, Embassy of the U.S.S.R., Washington, January 6, 1944, pp. 8-10.

11. Carl L. Becker, *How New Will the Better World Be?*, New York, Knopf, 1944, p. 241.
12. Norman Angell, *Let the People Know*, New York, Viking Press, 1943, pp. 85-88.
13. *Peace and War*, pp. 228-29. Italics mine.
14. *Ibid.*, p. 253.
15. Cf. Arnold Wolfers, "In Defense of the Small Countries," *Yale Review*, Winter, 1944, pp. 202-03, 217-18.
16. Secret protocol of November 15, 1818, Sir A. Alison, *Life of Lord Castlereagh*, Vol. III, p. 66, quoted in T. J. Lawrence, *Essays on Some Disputed Questions in Modern International Law*, Cambridge, Deighton Bell, 1884, p. 198.

CHAPTER X (pp. 156-62)

1. Cf. F. S. Dunn, *Peaceful Change*, New York, Council on Foreign Relations, 1937, Chapter V.
2. *A Working Peace System*, London, Royal Institute of International Affairs, 1943, p. 26.
3. Mitrany, *op. cit.*, argues for a functional development of international organization with the supra-national instruments developed function by function. *Contra*, see Commission to Study the Organization of Peace, "Fourth Report," *International Conciliation*, January, 1944, p. 8.

INDEX

Index

Adams, Henry, 12, 27, 73; on power politics as a game, 5-6; on collaboration with Germany and Russia, 73
Adler, Mortimer J., cited, 8 *n.*, 159 *n.*
Aggressor, probable identity of, 114, 151
"Aid to Britain," as aid to the United States, 37, 60, 65
Alaska, Panhandle boundary arbitration (1903), 29-30; and Russian-American relations, 79-80
Alison, A., cited, 173 *n.*
American Institute of Public Opinion, cited, 172 *n.*
America's security. *See* United States, security interest in Britain
Anderson, H. Foster, cited, 165 *n.*
Angell, Sir Norman, 148-49; cited, 167 *n.*, 169 *n.*, 173 *n.*
Anglo-American Caribbean Commission, 43 *n.*
Anglo-American leadership and colonial world, 43; avoidance of strategic vacuum, 48
Anglo-American relations, war-time interest in, 169 *n. See also* Great Britain and the United States
Anglo-Japanese alliance (1902), 14, 51-52
Anglo-Russian treaty (1907), 79
Anglo-Soviet defensive alliance (1942), 113, 133, 142-43, 157. *See also* Great Britain and the Soviet Union
Anglophobia, 31-33
Arab world, 35-36
Astor, Lady, 64
Atlantic Charter, 58, 121
Australia, interest in Anglo-American collaboration, 55
Australian Gallup Polls, cited, 55 *n.*

Austria-Hungary, disappearance as great power, 16
Aviation, postwar commercial, 35
Axis powers, diplomatic triumphs in the 1930's, 61; organization for winning short wars, 102

Balance of power, as sanction for peace based on preponderant power, 161; skill of early United States statesmen in analysis of, 4-5, 165 *n. See also* Power politics
Baldwin, Hanson W., cited, 81 *n.*
Balfour, Arthur, 30 *n;* commitment on Palestine, 35-36
Beard, Charles and Mary, cited, 6 *n.*, 135 *n.*
Becker, Carl, cited, 23 *n.* at 24, 148
"Belt of frontiers," Europe as, 95-96; Lord Curzon's conception of, 170 *n.*
Bemis, Samuel F., cited, 167 *n.*
Beneš, Eduard, 116, 118, 142
Beveridge, Albert, 63
Big Four, 18
Big Three, 12, 140, 147-48, 152
"Big Two," 101
Bingham, Alfred M., cited, 171 *n.*
Bipolar power system of postwar world, 97, 98
Bismarck, 15
Blitzkrieg, as nineteenth-century phenomenon, 21
"Blood" vs. "dollars" and Anglo-American misunderstanding, 37
Boer War, 55
Briand, Aristide, 171 *n.*
Britain. *See* Great Britain
British Commonwealth of Nations, dependence on United States support, 55-57

INDEX

Brodie, Bernard, cited, 166 *n*.
Burma Road, 135

Canada, interest in Anglo-American collaboration, 55-56; delayed entry into Second World War, 56. See also "Security union," United States-Canadian
Canning, 28
Carlson, J. R., cited, 168 *n*. at 169
Carr, E. H., cited, 171 *n*.
Castlereagh, Lord, 173 *n*.
Catlin, George, cited, 169 *n*.
Ceylon, self-government in, 46
Chamberlain, Joseph, 63
Chamberlin, William Henry, 84
Chandler, A. B., and retention of Pacific islets, 51; criticism of the Soviet Union, 81
China, great-power status, 18; as a regional power, 19-20; as "low-pressure" power area, 96 *n*., fragmentation of, as threat to super-power collaboration, 157 *n*.
Churchill, Winston, 20 *n*., 121 *n*.
Cleveland, Grover, 30 *n*.
Coalition for peace, 156. See also Three-power collaboration
Coalition peace strategy. See Three-power collaboration
Colegrove, Kenneth, 38, cited, 172 *n*.
Collaboration. See Three-power collaboration
Colonial peoples, interests of, 43-44
Colonial powers, responsibilities of, 45, and "have-not" powers, 47
Colonial world, government of, 44-46; and Anglo-American "race" superiority, 46-47; and Anglo-American domination of sea routes, 47-48
Combined Chiefs of Staff, 69, 156
"Command of the Atlantic" as basis for Anglo-American collaboration, 50
Commission to Study the Organization of Peace, cited, 173 *n*.

Commitments, United States' unwillingness to make, 62, 138, 149, 168 *n*.; and great-power collaboration, 148-49; to implement three-power collaboration, 156-57
Communist International, abolition of, 95, 127
Concert of Powers, 152
Connally resolution (1943), 133
Coudenhove-Kalergi, R. N., cited, 171 *n*.
Council of Asia, 20 *n*., 152-53
Council of Europe, 20 *n*., 152-53
Crowe, Sir Eyre, 15, 170 *n*.
Curzon, Lord, 170 *n*.
Czech-Soviet treaty of alliance (1943), 142, 171 *n*.

Dallin, David J., 84, cited, 87 *n*., 170 *n*., 171 *n*.
Dangerfield, R. J., cited, 168 *n*.
Davies, Lord, cited, 169 *n*., 171 *n*.
Davis, Elmer, 140
Davis, Forrest, 50, cited, 169 *n*.
Davis, Norman, 149
Declaration Regarding Italy (1943), 122, 123
Defense in depth, 86; as political concept, 113-14
Dickinson, Edwin D., cited, 172 *n*.
Disarmament, of Germany, 113-14; and compulsory nonparticipation in war, 136; as invitation to aggression, 136
Dobb, Maurice, cited, 170 *n*.
Dugdale, Blanche, cited, 30 *n*.
Dulles, Foster R., cited, 170 *n*.
Dunn, Frederick S., cited, 173 *n*.

Earle, Edward Mead, cited, 165 *n*., 166 *n*., 167 *n*.
Eastern and Central Europe, hegemony of the Soviet Union in, 82-83, 88, 92, 116, 119
Eastman, Max, 81
Economy of joint action, 130-39
"Empire" as symbol, 37

INDEX

Equality of states, under law, 143-44; and world organization, 144-46

Equilibrium zones, between Soviet and Anglo-American power, 96

Europe, outward migration of power from, 12-17; incapacity to solve own problems, 23; and the Soviet Union, comparison of population trends, 88-89; as "belt of frontiers" between U.S.S.R. and Western super-powers, 95-96; as chief arena of world politics, 109-10; integration of, 110, 112; indivisibility of security problem in, 113-14; not a natural unit for organization, 115-16. *See also* Eastern and Central Europe

European federation, 115, 171 *n*. *See also* Europe, integration of

Federalist, 165 *n*.

"Federal union," 65

Finland, Winter War with Soviet Union, 80-81; as Hitler's ally, 94

First World War, American involvement in, 32-33, 134, 168 *n*.

Fish, C. R., cited, 167 *n*.

Foreign policy, necessity for basing on multiple contingencies, 74-75

"Four freedoms," 126

France, De Gaullist, 17; as a regional power, 19; as bridgehead, 132

Franco-British Financial Agreement of December (1939), 65

Franco-Soviet defensive alliance (1935), 148

"Friendly regimes," Soviet insistence upon in border areas, 82, 93-94; and Soviet security sphere, 94, 116-17

Garvin, J. L., 64

Gelber, Lionel, 30 *n*., 63; cited, 165 *n*., 167 *n*., 169 *n*.

General security organization, 9, 114-15, 147-48, 153-54

General war, participation of great powers in, 138 *n*. *See also* Third World War

Geneva Disarmament Conference (1934), 149

German power, revival of, 103, 104

German problem, necessity for three-power agreement on, 97, 112-15

Germany, rise of as great power, 15; as a world power, British opposition to, 15; as a regional power, 20; political hegemony and intra-European trade, 42; nonaggression pact with the Soviet Union, 77, 87; Soviet interest in bolshevization, 87-88; and tripolar organization of world politics, 97-99; bid for European hegemony after 1960, 104; "middle-run" improvement in power position relative to Western powers, 105; advantage of geographic position, 105; disarmament of, 113; as "most probable" aggressor, 114, 151; postwar government of, 124-25; and "sin" of Versailles, 159-60

Gibbs, Philip, cited, 169 *n*.

Good Neighbor policy, 7

Grafton, Samuel, 3

Grain production, surplus, 35

Grattan, C. Hartley, cited, 168 *n*.

Great Britain, as first world power, 13, 166 *n*.; end of splendid isolation, 16; extra-European alliances, 28-29; attitudes toward the United States, 31; declining role in world affairs, 38-39, 166 *n*.; status as first-rank power, 57; dependence on Dominions, 57; declining power position of, 57 *n*.; as American "advanced base," 57-58; as "sole buyer" of American military might, 58; dependence of the United States on her Empire, 58; demand for postwar commitments from the United States, 62; unilateral dec-

laration regarding American position in Western Pacific, 69, 156
Great Britain and Russia, nineteenth century conflict, 78
Great Britain and the Soviet Union, common policy in opposition to Germany, 79. *See also* Anglo-Soviet defensive alliance
Great Britain and United States, war between, 27, 29, 49, 52, 167 *n.*; historic controversies, 27-32; United States hegemony in New World, 28-30; present friction between, 33-36; barriers to co-operation, 36-39; sea power in colonial world, 47-48; strategic interdependence, 50-69; common values, 50-51; naval rivalry between, 52-54; opposition to aggression, 54-55; complementary military assets, 58-59; allocation of responsibilities between, 59-61; and Germany's neighbors, 62-63; collaboration with Soviet Union, 62-63, 74-75; anti-Anglo-American coalition, 63-64; and Soviet fear of encirclement, 64; question of Anglo-American alliance, 66-67; alternatives to alliance, 67-68; as single power-nucleus, 73-74. *See also* Three-power collaboration
Great-power status, of France, Germany, Italy, China, and Japan, 17-20; military and moral criteria, 18
Great Powers, and power politics, 3-4; in Europe, 12; and non-European powers, 14-15; after First World War, 16-17; as the significant "selves" in international politics, 76 *n.*; participation in general war, 138 *n.*; common interest in preventive aggression, 141; collective action and small-power protection, 141-42; interest in spontaneous small-power co-operation, 152

Hague Conference (1907), 145
Halifax, Lord, 57 *n.*
Hambro, C. J., 142, 143
Hamilton, Alexander, 4-5, cited, 165 *n.*
Harvey, W. B., 158 *n.* at 159
"Have-not" nations, desire for colonies, 47; vs. "have" nations, 54
Hay, John, 5, 27, 167-68 *n.*
Hay-Pauncefote Treaties, 167 *n.*
Hearst, William Randolph, 64
Heartland, 78, 131
Herriot, Eduard, 148-49
Hicks, F. C., cited, 172 *n.*
Holtzendorff, Franz, cited, 172 *n.*
Holy Alliance, 79
Hoover, Herbert, 41
Howe, Quincy, 32-33; cited, 172 *n.*
Hull, Cordell, 147 *n.*, 150 *n.*; unwillingness to commit United States, 134-35

Ideological intervention, 80
Independence for colonial areas, 44-46; "timetables" for, 45
India, as barrier to Anglo-American understanding, 36-37; independence, 45; and Philippines, comparison of positions of, 45-46
International government, "democratic" organization of, 144-45
International organization. *See* General security organization
International police force. *See* Supranational police force
Internationalists, 6
Interventionists, 7
Islands for War Debts Committee, 168-69 *n.*
Isolationism, feasibility for great powers, 129-30; expectation of, 132-35
Isolationists, 6
Italy, as least of great powers, 16; as first ex-enemy power, 122

INDEX

Japan, rise of, 14; as a regional power, 20; in First World War, 52 *n.*
Jay Treaty (1794), 51
Jefferson, Thomas, 4
Jennings, W. Ivor, cited, 171 *n.*
Joesten, Joachim, cited, 93 *n.*, 170 *n.*, 171 *n.*

Knorr, K. E., cited, 33 *n.* at 34
Knox, Capt. Dudley W., cited, 169 *n.*
Korneichuk, Alexander, 82

Lasswell, Harold D., 76 *n.*, cited, 165 *n.*
Latin America, British investments in, 34
Lawrence, T. J., cited, 173 *n.*
League of Nations, Shatrov's criticism of, 146; and disputes between small powers, 154
Lehman, Herbert H., 40
Leith-Ross, Sir Frederick, 40
Lend-lease, as aid to Britain, 37; pressure for repayment, 51; as bargaining weapon in Anglo-American relations, 51; and Anglo-American collaboration, 65
"Liberation nationalism," 44
"Life line of Empire," Russian threat to, 78
Lippmann, Walter, 5, 23 *n.*, 53, 156, 166 *n.*, 167 *n.*
List, Friedrich, 166 *n.*, 167 *n.*
Locarno Pact, 113-14

MacArthur, General Douglas, 22, 59
MacCormac, John, cited, 169 *n.*
McCormick, Robert R., 33 *n.*
MacDonald, Ramsay, 148-49
Mackinder, Sir Halford, 78, 131-32
McKinley, William, 165 *n.*
Manchurian crisis, 61 *n.*
Markets, in semi-colonial areas, 35
Mead, Margaret, 7 *n.*, cited, 171 *n.*
Menefee, Selden, cited, 172 *n.*
Military power, loss of efficiency when transmitted to distant points, 22; relativity of, 101, 102; non-quantitative aspects, 102. *See also* Power
Millis, Walter, 135 *n.*, cited, 168 *n.*
Mitrany, David, 158, cited, 173 *n.*
Monroe, James, 28
Monroe Doctrine, 28, 68, 165 *n.*
Morgan, J. P., 32
Moscow Declaration, 18, 67, 83, 84, 126, 130 *n.*, 133-34, 152, 153, 158
Motherwell, Hiram, cited, 168 *n.*
Mountbatten, Lord Louis, 59
Mowat, R. B., cited, 169 *n.*
Munich Pact, 61, 142, 148

National Committee of Free Germany, 88, 123-24
National Opinion Research Center, cited, 137 *n.*
Neumann, Sigmund, cited, 99 *n.*, 168 *n.*
New Zealand, interest in Anglo-American collaboration, 55; solidarity with Britain, 169 *n.*
Non-European powers, as great powers, 14; and settlement of Europe, 23
Notestein, Frank, 88-89; cited, 171 *n.*
Nye committee hearings, cited, 168 *n.*

Ogdensburg Agreement (1940), 56 *n.*
Olney, Richard, 14, 30, 63, 141

"Pacific First" strategy, as mask for Anglophobia, 33, 33 *n.*; and postwar Anglo-American collaboration in Southeast Asia, 48 *n.*
Padover, Saul K., cited, 150 *n.*
Palmer, Frederick, cited, 168 *n.*
Pan-Slavism, 79, 87
Palestine, 35-36
Pascal, 9
Peaceful change, 157-58
Peripheral powers, super-powers as, 21-22, 109
Permanent peace, 8 *n.*, 159

INDEX

Philippines and India, comparison of positions of, 45
Poland, alliance with Soviet Union, 118; Polish Ukraine, 117-18. *See also* Union of Polish Patriots
Polar opposites in the postwar world, 97, 99
Polignac memorandum, 28, 167 *n.*
Polish National Council, 88
Population trends, Europe and the Soviet Union, 88-89
Power, in postwar world, 3; as scoring device, 6, 165 *n.*; uses of, 8-11; distribution of, 12-24; irrelevance as index of influence in welfare problems, 158. *See also* Military power. Power politics
Power politics, definition of, 4; as a game, 5-6; impossibility of escape from, 7
Pringle, H. F., cited, 165 *n.*

Race, and Anglo-American leadership in colonial world, 46-47; and an anti-Anglo-American coalition, 63-64
Railroad, and shifting balance of power, 15, 21, 166 *n.*
Reconstruction, as Anglo-American task, 39; political implications of credits for, 43; of Soviet devastated areas, 85
Regional powers, 19, 20, 153
Rehabilitation, as Anglo-American task, 42-43
Relief, as Anglo-American task, 39-41; political implications of, 41
Rimland, consolidation of, 103
Roosevelt, Franklin D., 56 *n.*, 68, 134, 136, 149
Roosevelt, Theodore, 5, 30 *n.*, 129, 165 *n.*
Root, Elihu, 144
Rowe, David N., cited, 18 *n.*, 157 *n.*
Rubber, United States postwar supply of, 33
Russia, as *bête noire* of British diplomacy, 73, 78. *See also* Soviet Union

Salisbury, Lord, 29-30
Savage, M. J., 169 *n.*
Security, power for the sake of, 11; colonial, 45. *See also* United States, security interest in Britain
Security organization. *See* General security organization
Security spheres, and Anglo-Russian-American collaboration, 96-97
"Security union," United States-Canadian, 11, 56 *n.*, 76 *n.*
Separation, of major centers of power, 21-23, 76, 102, 103, 112
Shatrov, B., cited, 146
Shipping and shipbuilding, surplus capacity, 34
Slosson, Preston, cited, 169 *n.*
Small powers, in a world dominated by great powers, 3-4; as makeweights for stability, 112; conflict of interest with great powers, 140-41; interest in three-power collaboration, 141; and a single great neighbor, 141; and collective great-power actions, 141; and "undemocratic" three-power collaboration, 143; right to equal protection under law, 143-44; theoretical interest in equality, 145-46; as collaborators of great powers in enforcing security, 151-52; coercion in nonpolitical disputes, 158 *n.*; viability of, 171 *n.*
Smuts, Jan C., 19 *n.*, 57 *n.*
Sovereignty, fears of sacrifice of, 148
Soviet-American friendship, influence of geography on, 80
Soviet security sphere, in Eastern and Central Europe, 116-17, 120; in Far East, 117 *n. See also* "Friendly regimes"

Soviet Union, task of reconstruction, 39; sensitivity to political implications of relief, 41; fear of encirclement, 64; calculation of risks regarding future policy, 74-75; encouragement of nonexpansionist forces in, 77; as "pariah" power, 77; pact with Hitlerite Germany, 77, 87; Winter War with Finland, 80-81, 94; fear of great anti-Soviet coalition, 81-82; requirement of "friendly regimes" in border areas, 82, 93-94; hegemony in Eastern and Central Europe, 82-83, 88, 92, 119; decentralization of conduct of foreign affairs, 84, 93, 96; collaboration not to be assumed, 85, 90; evidence of moderation in foreign policy of, 85-90; eastward gravitation of Soviet industry, 86; nonexpansionist forces in, 86-87; interest in Sovietized Germany, 87-88; trends in population increase, 88-89; annexations (1939-41), 93-94; postwar interests in Western Europe, 95; threat value to United States, 101-103; and revived German power, 104-105; extent of intervention in Eastern and Central Europe, 119; "good neighbor" policy, 120; collaboration with Germany, 171 *n.*

Soviet Union and Great Britain. *See* Great Britain and Soviet Union

Soviet Union and the United States, sensitivity to steps in each other's foreign policy, 76; disputes based on contrasting ideologies, 80; not necessarily polar opposites, 99; possibility of war between, 100-101

Soviet Union and Western powers. *See* Western powers and Soviet Union

Sprout, Harold and Margaret, cited, 166 *n.*, 169 *n.*

Spykman, Nicholas J., cited, 169 *n.*, 170 *n.* at 171

Stalin, Joseph, 29, 92, 170 *n.*

Stimson, Henry P., 61 *n.*

Strachey, John, 65

Strategic vacuum, in colonial world, 45, 48

Strausz-Hupé, Robert, cited, 170 *n.*

Streit, Clarence, cited, 169 *n.*

Super-power collaboration. *See* three-power collaboration

Super-powers, as world powers, 20-21; as peripheral powers, 21; strategic map of world of, 96; interest in preventing consolidation of Europe, 111-12; as "powers of general interest," 152 *n.*

Supra-national police force, 9, 153, 154

Suvich, Fulvio, 134

Symbols, convergence of key words in political vocabulary of three super-powers, 121-22

Tansill, C. C., cited, 167 *n.*

Teheran Declaration, 64 *n.*, 83-84, 121

Temperley, H. W. V., 152 *n.*

Territorial aggrandizement, opposition in United States to, 75

"Threat value," 76; of Soviet Union to United States, 101-103

Third World War, 98, 101, 103, 105

Thomas, T. H., cited, 166 *n.*

Three-power collaboration, 109; and security spheres, 96-97; necessity for agreement on Germany, 97, 112-15, 120-21; and interests of Europe, 110-12; and nonconsolidation of Europe, 115; and anti-Fascist democracy, 116; efficiency of, 131-33; and "democratic" world organization, 143; and general international organization, 147-48; voluntary basis of, 148; framework of commitments, 156-

57; deficiencies of, 157-60; and permanent peace, 160; *New Yorker's* objections to, 166 *n*. *See also* Economy of joint action

Trade policies, Anglo-American conflict over, 34

Tripolar organization of world politics in 1930's, 99; in event of revival of German power, 103; as alternative to peace based on preponderant power, 106

Twenty-One Demands, 52 *n*.

"Unconditional surrender," 121

Union of Polish Patriots, 82, 88, 94, 117-19

U.S.S.R. *See* Soviet Union

United Nations Relief and Rehabilitation Administration (UNRRA), 40

United States, and "Europe's quarrels," 4-5, 60-62; attitude toward power politics, 6-7; as great power and as world power, 13-17; hostile attitudes in, toward Great Britain, 31-33; and British Commonwealth, 55-57; security interest in Britain, 57-59, 67-69; "no prior commitments" as policy toward Europe, 62, 138; unilateral declaration of interest in Britain's independent existence, 68, 156; and future Soviet foreign policy, 106; political implications of exports, 126-27; public opinion on postwar international collaboration, 137; minimum participation in postwar world politics, 139; unwillingness to make commitments, 149, 168 *n*.

United States and Great Britain. *See* Great Britain and United States

United States and Russia, historic friendship, 79-80

United States and the Soviet Union. *See* Soviet Union and the United States

United States Constitution, and foreign affairs, 133, 172 *n*.

United States Senate, role in foreign affairs, 38, 133, 168 *n*.

Universities Committee on Post-war International Problems, cited, 172 *n*.

Vagts, Alfred, cited, 28, 52, 165 *n*., 167 *n*.

Van Cauwelaert, Frans, 109, 115

Van Kirk, Walter, cited, 7 *n*.

Venezuela, boundary dispute with Great Britain (1895), 29-30

Viner, Jacob, 158 *n*.

Vyshinsky, Andrei, 95

Washington Conference of 1922, 16-17, 52-53; and no fortifications agreement in Western Pacific, 53

Wasilewska, Wanda, 82

Weinfeld, Abraham, cited, 171 *n*.

Welfare activities, dependence on security, 158

Welles, Sumner, cited, 166 *n*.

Werner, Max, 94, 131

Western powers and Soviet Union, separation of main centers of power, 22-23, 76, 102-103; war between, 103

Westlake, J., 145

Whitaker, A. P., cited, 167 *n*.

Wilhelm II of Germany, 15

Wilson, Woodrow, 30 *n*., 41 *n*., 150

Wolfers, Arnold, cited, 113 *n*., 166 *n*., 171 *n*., 172 *n*.

World powers, rise of Great Britain, United States, and Soviet Union as, 13-17; super-powers as, 20-21

Wright, Q., cited, 136 *n*., 138 *n*.

Yugow, A., cited, 170 *n*.